AF378760

The
Sedona
Man
The Life and Adventures of Arizona Cowboy
BOB BRADSHAW
As told by Bob Bradshaw
with Kathleen Francis

HORSE INDEX

Look for these other fine publications by Bob Bradshaw:

Sedona Red Rock Country

Television, Commercials & Movies of the Southwest

Westerns of the Red Rock Country

Indian Country Land of the Navajo

The Arizona Book

Four Seasons of Sedona

Weird Rock Formations

Verde Valley Arizona's Hidden Treasure

Author's Notes

My purpose in writing this autobiography was to document not only my life but a portion of the Southwest's history. I wish to express my appreciation to Kathleen Francis, my editor and book producer, and to Karen Reider, my designer, for their contribution to this book. I am basically a man with a simple nature who became a genuine Arizona cowboy. While often challenged with hardships through some of America's most difficult years, I still managed to live a life of my own choosing. The tales of my adventures have been spoken to hundreds of eager visitors and locals alike. I guess I'm considered one of Sedona's storytellers of long standing. My lineage continues the family heritage of honoring the beauty of the area and contributing to the development of a balanced formula of commerce while protecting the precious land we all cherish. I arrived on this sacred land when there were 300 people and a well from which we collected water for our family and livestock. I have witnessed growth here for almost 60 years, sometimes with wonder, often with sadness. This is my story and the story of Sedona.

Bob Bradshaw

Bob Bradshaw stands tall as an American treasure in his own right. It has been my pleasure to be part of the development and production of his work. I have enjoyed the companionship with him and the pleasure of many long hours on the land photographing together the extraordinary terrain of Sedona and the Verde Valley. I have edited this book with care in keeping his voice and his requests for what he wanted to depict as his life in Sedona, the town he considers to be the best place in the world to live. We hope you enjoy this slice of Arizona's colorful past.

Kathleen Francis

©2002 All rights reserved. No part of this book may be reproduced in any form, except by a newspaper or magazine reviewer who wishes to quote brief passages in connection with a review.

Published by
Bradshaw Enterprises
P.O. Box 20062
Sedona, Arizona 86341

All photos from the private collection of
Bob Bradshaw ©2002

Type, layout, design by Karen Reider & Mike Jung
Editing & Production by Kathleen Francis

Printing Coordinated by PRHollywood

Printed in Korea

Because my life has been predominantly viewed through a photo lens, my autobiography will follow the adage "one picture is worth a thousand words". In truth, this autobiography is more like a journey through the photo album of my life. Basically, I am a simple man of few words with a deep appreciation for nature. And though as a young boy I displayed artistic talent in drawing, I gravitated to photography and chose the majestic red rock formations of Sedona and the surrounding Arizona grandeur as my primary palette. I was blessed with an innate ability, an eye for composition. And in my heart, I know that with each "click" of my camera, I'm never alone in my viewfinder. Even now well into my eighties, I'm just as enthusiastic to see what surprises have developed out of each new roll of film. Although I started my photographic career at the age of twelve, it's still exciting to me to share the great photographic moments I was able to capture over a span of seven decades.

My family history began with rather unusual circumstances. My Father, John Bradshaw, and my Uncle Marion both attended Hiram College in Ohio. They were exceptional athletes and were selected for the Hiram College Hall of Fame in all sports; baseball, football, basketball and track. High in the bleachers watching this young champion athlete was a lovely liberal arts student, Ruth Chapman, who kept her eye on more than the ball. Ruth and John became Mr. & Mrs. Bradshaw on September 12, 1916. As a result of my Father's athletic skills, the YMCA offered my Father a position as a physical education instructor in China. So this young, newly married couple packed their bags and their dreams and headed for a very different world. As a result of this unconventional situation, I was born on June 9, 1918 not on American soil, but in Amoy, China. Dad's abilities as a coach proved to be as exceptional as his personal performance. While in China, he trained his Chinese students and took them to the Philippines to compete in The World Games. They proudly won the Decathlon for China. During the four-year stay in China, my sisters, Holly and Ruth Esther, were also born. In 1922, we returned to America by ship and my Dad went to work for the YMCA in Cleveland, Ohio. Until the age of four, I knew only one language…Chinese, which I learned from my Chinese amah who looked after me in Amoy. My mother told me my amah cried for days when she learned we were returning to the states. I must have been quite an anomaly as my parents arrived back in America. I learned English in school. Still today, I have the dubious distinction of being the only cowpuncher in the world that can sing "Jesus Loves Me" in Chinese.

My baby sister had her first birthday at Grandma's house on the eastside of Cleveland, when we were living at 2058 Lewis Drive in Lakewood, a suburb of Cleveland. Our house was the first one built on our street. We used to hang out around the construction crews watching the neighborhood develop. The basements, which everyone had in Cleveland, were dug out by horses pulling fresnos. A fresno, if you didn't know, is a big metal dirt scooper pulled by a horse. The big construction equipment wasn't around in those days.

I lived an almost Huckleberry Finn childhood combing the land and exploring. One day, another boy and I went to the railroad tracks, miles from our house on Lewis Drive. While we were playing, we discovered a man lying beside a railroad car. He didn't look like he was breathing, but we were too scared to get close, so we climbed to the top of the railroad car and threw rocks at him thinking that if he was asleep, the rocks might wake him. He still didn't move, so we ran all the way home as fast as we could. My mother called the police and we showed them where he was. Later, we read an article in the newspaper, which mentioned that two small boys found a dead man. It also said that he died from drinking wood alcohol. At that age, this experience was particularly traumatic for me and my friend. I suspect that this incident

Mom and Dad holding me

The Chinese Hospital where I was born

A Chinese Birthday Gathering – I'm sitting in the chair at the right

Mom and me

Mom and Dad in rickshaws on the streets of Shanghai

As a baby, I drank Water Buffalo milk. I credit that diet with the fact that now in my 80s, I still have all my own teeth and have never broken any bone except in my feet when a horse jumped on me.

This was my first horse-back ride

Two years old in China

Holly and me on the beach

My home in Lakewood, Ohio

Mom, Ruth Esther, and me aboard a ship
coming home from China

My handsome Dad

We were lined up
on my dad in this picture,
back in the States

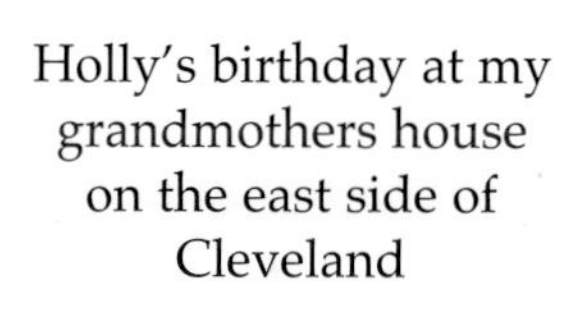

Holly's birthday at my
grandmothers house
on the east side of
Cleveland

created repulsion to alcohol in me, which was actually a positive life decision produced from a very dark situation.

As a kid growing up, I hated school mostly because it kept me away from the fields, woods and streams near our house. I developed an intense magnetism towards nature. School for me was a waste of precious daytime hours that could be spent outdoors. My mother, aware of my inclinations, bought me a book called *The Field Book of Insects,* which sparked my interest in collecting butterflies and moths. My disdain for school didn't interfere with my enjoyment of reading; I loved to study things that interested me. Another book she gave me on reptiles initiated my huge collection of snakes, which filled our basement along with owls and chipmunks. I once tried to catch a flying squirrel only to discover that it didn't take kindly to being captured; it let me know by sinking its teeth mightily into my hand! My mother grew more careful in her selection of reading material directed my way since the consequences dramatically affected her environment.

About this same time in my life, my mother bought me a book called *The B Bar X Boys on the Ranch.* I'm certain the reading of that book sparked the fire in me to be a rancher someday. My cow brand today is ∽ **2** (Lazy S Two) and my horse brand is **9\2** (Nine Bar Two). Having read and reread that book, the power of early influence on the future events of our lives in my case seems pretty evident. Who could predict that a kid from Cleveland would seek such a different path for himself filled with adventure, hardships and fulfillment of childhood dreams?

The backdrop of my life has small, savored stories that warm my heart as I recall them. If you remember some of the same things I do, you must be about as old as I am. If you don't have a clue what I'm talking about at times, you have an opportunity to wonder and find out how different life was just 70 years ago.

The familiar sounds of the horse-drawn milk wagon and the junk peddler's wagon calling, "Paper rag!" is a dusty memory of my childhood. The peddlers would buy your old newspapers and used goods. Milk came in bottles and the cream settled at the top until we shook it up. Margarine was white and if you wanted it yellow you had to mix it with a capsule of colored fluid.

Before there were speakers or radios, we would fight for the earphones to hear programs on the crystal sets. When we finally got a radio with a speaker, our favorite programs were comedian, Joe Penner, and the thriller, *I Love a Mystery*, starring Mercedes McCambridge. I never imagined that later in my life I would work with her on a picture called *Johnny Guitar* filmed in Sedona in which I rode with Ward Bond chasing the "bad guys".

Like a period movie, pleasant memories replay like going to the corner for an ice cream cone. I'd plunk down my 3 cents for a 14-inch long Ice Cream cone that I still miss to this day. We'd look forward all week to go to the movies on Saturday. For 10 cents, we'd watch Hop-a-long Cassidy and Tom Mix westerns till the cows came home.

Traveling was a big deal. We went to Bangor, Maine, Washington, D.C., and Gettysburg, Pennsylvania driving very carefully in my dad's old car. Seeing the National Air Races at the Cleveland Airport was great fun. The pilots raced their planes around the pylons to a crowd of amazed onlookers. Seeing the Graf Zeppelin and other dirigibles flying over our house became a common sight. One of the most memorable moments of my youth was at Cleveland Airport. I was standing about 100 feet from Charles Lindberg when he flew in with his plane – The Spirit of St. Louis. This and watching Babe Ruth play at the stadium were exciting things for a kid my age to experience. When Babe Ruth came to bat, there was pandemonium in the park. I always dreamed of catching one of his home-run balls.

Dad took this picture on our trip to Maine. Mom, me, Ruth and Holly.

Boating at Hunky Dory

We spent our vacations at Uncle Al's
Hunky Dory farm. They made this
playhouse cabin just for us kids.
I was at the top of this tree
(right side of picture) and almost fell out.
I have been afraid of heights ever since.

I spent hours drawing my sister,
Holly, in our back yard.

Like most kids, I disliked my assigned chores like cutting the lawn and going to the icehouse with a wagon to haul back a block of ice for our icebox (before electric refrigerators came along). We had a Maytag washer with a wringer on it. In the winter, I had the job of shoveling coal into the furnace in the basement and hauling away the ashes. Washing dishes was no fun either because it was a long time before detergent soap was discovered and nothing seemed to ever get clean. When I reflect on these events and realize how much has changed, I wonder if I recorded enough on the celluloid ribbon strewn down Memory Lane.

Summer vacation usually found us at "Hunky Dory," my Uncle Al's farm near Alliance, Ohio. That's where I learned to swim. We were old enough to pitch in and pick the raspberries for market. Like a lot of kids our age, we were fearless. I climbed a tall tree by the cabin, slipped and very nearly fell to my death. That incident gave me a fear of heights to this day. We sometimes did dangerous things like waiting at a snowy corner for a car to stop and then grabbing the bumper for a sled ride. Summer found me on a different vehicle, my bike, with the same dangerous scenario catching a ride by holding onto a streetcar or a truck. Once, a disgruntled truck driver got rid of me by pulling over to the curb. Needless to say, that wrecked my bike, but I didn't get hurt all that much.

When I was a kid, I always thought that if I wanted to find out what was on the moon I would have to live to the year 2000. Boy, was I wrong! After all, the Wright Brothers made the first flight in 1903. To think a man walked on the moon by 1969 is rather astonishing.

In 1932 and 1934, the family went to Howdenvale, Ontario. This was heaven for my Dad since he loved to fish. I kept myself busy creating my own amusements. I made myself something to ride out of a pipe and two wagon wheels. We had a great time and got a lot of attention with it. Since we were there on the lake, I made a small sailboat out of an old rowboat that my friends and I spent hours maneuvering ourselves from one end of the lake to another. With today's modern technology, the motivation for this kind of creativity seems to be lost in the world of computer games and cyberspace. I often feel the appreciation and rewards of being outdoors is lost for today's youth. Progress has its price in ways that can cripple parts of what it means to be a human being, part of the whole experience of embracing our rich and beautiful planet.

My talent for drawing developed while I was growing up in Lakewood. When I was twelve, I drew a color pencil picture of an imaginary underwater scene and took first place in a national contest sponsored by Eberhard Faber Color Pencils. That same year, I received a free camera from Eastman Kodak Company. Anyone who turned 12 years of age in June of that year got a free camera. Thanks to that Kodak promotion, my interest in photography took birth. You hold a portion of that body of work in your hands. Beginning in 1950, a major part of my living was earned from photography. I was a major contributor to Arizona Highways Magazine for 35 years.

My father continued to nurture young athletes as I completed my teenage years. Among some of his most rewarding efforts was his impressive development of one of the world's most extraordinary Olympic competitors, Jesse Owens. My father trained Jesse at our high school track in Cleveland. Jesse ran every day on that track. Some of my fondest memories were tagging along with my Dad to watch this exceptional athlete in the making. 1936 was the year Jesse Owens made headlines in the Olympics for America. He won four gold metals; the hundred-meter dash, the two hundred meter dash, 4x100 meter relay and the long jump. Owens's performances in the two hundred meter and long jump were Olympic records, while the relay team broke a world record. Adolf Hitler planned the '36 games in Berlin as a demonstration of Aryan supremacy. It was rumored at the time that to have a black athlete, son of a sharecropper and grandson of a slave, defeat the Germans, caused Hitler to consider suicide.

I used a stuffed bird as a model and my imagination for the rest.

I drew this from my imagination - It won first place in the National Eberhard Faber contest.

I drew this one in black and white and added the treasure chest.

More from my wild imagination!

Besides this, 1936 marked a number of important events in my life. I bought my first 35 mm camera, an Argus with a hefty price tag of $12.50. I learned how to develop film and make prints. My contemporaries have commented that many of the pictures I took in the 30's are as good as those taken by professionals with hi-tech equipment today. That same year, I graduated from Lakewood High School. I took a job at the YMCA camp for the summer as a craft instructor (wood, leather and metal work). After my summer job, I took on work feeling my way into what I liked and didn't like. The job I hated most was running an elevator at the Lakeview Hotel in Rocky River. Running a close second was working as a grocery clerk. I also worked two seasons picking apples at Neal's fruit farm, which was hard work, but at least it kept me outside. Apple knocking is no picnic.

I have often noted the similarity of my roots and that of Zane Grey, who also hailed from Ohio. He too loved the outdoors more than anything. He wrote the words, I took the pictures. At a crossroads in his life, he had to decide whether he wanted to be a baseball player in the major leagues or stay with his writing. Fortunate for us, he chose the latter. Some of his words are particularly poignant to me. *The waterways through the woods took possession of me. Larks and swamp blackbirds, orioles and cardinals were everywhere. Autumn passed and winter came and cold filled me with disgust and discomfort that only the remembered joy of summer and idle days could alleviate.* On that, we couldn't be more alike, and this next quote finds us also in agreement. *At church, I liked the singing, but the preacher's long, dry rigamarole was something terrific to endure.* - Zane Grey His autobiography is one of my favorite books to this day.

I always dreamt of finding a place in the west with a ranch. So I made it my goal to travel around until I found a place that I liked. Cleveland has a terrible climate, hot in the summer and unbearably cold in the winter. So the first chance I got, I bummed a ride to Florida and spent the next three winters as a truck farmer. I picked up potatoes and loaded them on trucks for 10 cents an hour (no room & board). I pulled vegetables and took them to Miami for market working a ten-hour day for a dollar. While this doesn't sound like much money, in those days, $3.00 could buy your groceries for a week. I did most of this work in Goulds, a town between Miami and Homestead, where the warm Gulf Stream came in close and the days and nights were beautifully warm.

I will never forget my first trip to Florida from Ohio. When I was in Cleveland, I had to have my antrums (lower sinuses) cleaned out everyday. It was terribly painful. One heavenly January day when I was in Orlando, Florida, as I was walking up the steps of the post office, the sun felt particularly wonderful. I just sat there for a while, as the heat of the sun seemed to penetrate through every pore. And suddenly, my sinus problems completely disappeared. For me it seemed like a miracle and an end to a painful, chronic condition.

Back in Cleveland, my chance to head out west finally came when I got a job driving in a caravan of Dodge trucks and Plymouth cars. In 1939, most new vehicles were driven to various parts of the country. Our route started at the factory in Detroit and ended up in Phoenix, Arizona. This was before bigrig auto-transport trucks were designed. Fifteen of us each drove a Dodge pickup and pulled a Plymouth car behind. In that entire caravan, I was the only driver who didn't jack knife the truck into the headlights of the car or bang up the vehicles in some other way. I was also the only driver who could follow the route signs. The highway systems at that time were hardly what they are today and getting confused was commonplace. The caravan leader had to find all of the drivers when they got lost on some city street. We were supposed to stay one telephone pole apart so we wouldn't get lost. At one point in the trip, the guy ahead

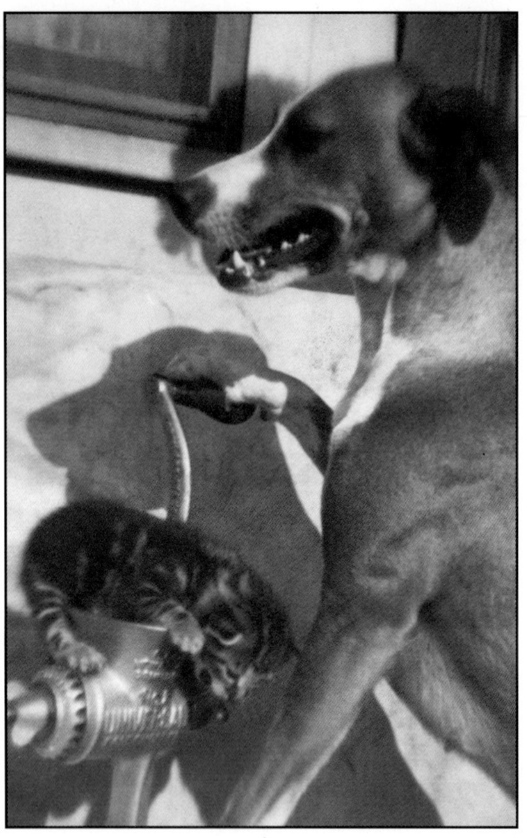

Wags seemed to have a good time
performing these stunts.

I set up a little darkroom in the basement of our house in Lakewood. This print of Wags below was the first one to come out of the developer.

Wags, the dog

*My pets
didn't always get
along.*

*The dog didn't get
skunked.
My camera and
I did!*

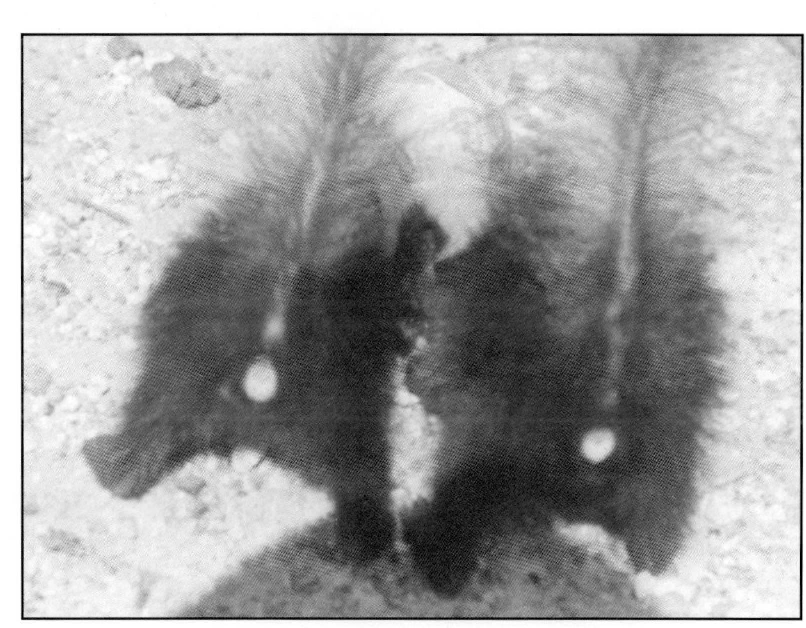

My mother may have regretted giving
me books on reptiles and insects.
Our basement was a managerie of captured species.

On the Florida coast near Miami

A photo I took of a pelican
on our trip to Florida.

My packsack and bed-roll.
The rain shield and mosquito net
was my idea.

I was the instructor of the YMCA camp near Chagrim Falls, Ohio. That's me standing on the left, my boss is on the right. We taught woodworking, metal work and leather work.

Apple knocking was no picnic!

I pulled beets on a truck farm in Florida.

Ohio Canal – A beautiful composition for a teenage boy

I took this photograph of Niagra Falls with my Argus Camera.

of me stopped to pick up a drunken hitchhiker and then headed out again. We were all very tired with only one night's sleep in four days. The guy up ahead put the hitchhiker in the car he was towing. The drunk curled up on the seat of the Plymouth. A few miles farther on, the driver got sleepy. I saw him go into the left ditch, wake up and pull back onto the road flipping the towed car upside down. Maybe the booze helped the hitchhiker to survive unharmed. Anyway, we finally came to the last stretch on the fifth night, passing the Superstition Mountains near Phoenix. I remember beating my head against the side of the truck to keep awake.

After we were paid in Phoenix, I caught a ride to California and hopped a freight train to Sacramento. From there, I caught a Union Pacific freight headed for Ogden, Utah. Somewhere in the desert between Sacramento and Ogden, I fell asleep in a reefer (a boxcar where ice was placed to refrigerate the cars). While I was sleeping, they pulled off on a siding to eliminate some of the cars. Fortunately for me, a brakeman came along and checked the reefer I was sleeping in before he locked the lid. I would have been cooked alive in there if he had not checked it. I transferred to the part of the train that continued on through Utah. Part of my journey allowed me to see the Great Salt Lake as the tracks sliced their way through the middle of it. It was quite an experience. My luck ran out for free passage when I got to the Ogden freight yards and tried to catch a freight to Grand Junction, Colorado. At the Ogden yards they had three railroad detectives (called "bulls" by the hobos) checking every freight that was leaving. One "bull" would ride the train near the engine as it pulled out, one near the middle and one at the caboose. The "bulls" would stay on the train until the cars got going too fast for a man to jump on, then *they* would jump off to remain at the location.

One of the most embarrassing times is when I got caught trying to get on and I was told to buy a ticket out of state on a passenger train or go to jail for 20 days. Not wanting to spend time in jail, I gave my last $10 for a ticket to Grand Junction, Colorado. They made *sure* that I did buy that ticket by following me to the ticket booth in the station.

When I arrived in Grand Junction, I was worse off than when I was in Ogden. The railroad yard was bigger and employed a lot of detectives. I learned that the highway patrol was on the lookout for transients too, so I waited until dark and caught a big truck into Rifle, Colorado. I spent the night rolled up in my sleeping bag and stepped out to the highway the next morning. My luck started to get better because as I was stepping into a car that was giving me a ride, one of the patrol cars pulled up behind. If I had still been on the road, I would have been picked up for vagrancy because I had no money left at all. The kind people in the car took me to Glenwood Springs, a town that, I was to learn, had no "bulls" in the train yard, so I managed to catch a freight train bound for Denver.

I was on my bedroll lying on a flatcar loaded with big lead blocks looking up at the Royal Gorge. There was never a dull moment riding the rails. I fell asleep before we got to the 8-mile long Moffett Tunnel and when I woke up, I was covered with soot from the engine. The train was headed down the mountain into Denver. The car I was riding on was full of lead. It was also near the caboose, so I could see the entire train snaking down the mountain below me. I will never forget that beautiful sight.

When I got to Denver, I called a friend who put me up for awhile. His sister was trying to get me a job on a ranch, but times were still hard and nobody would give me a job. My friend, Lowell, loaned me $12 and I made my way thumbing back to Michigan where my folks had a cabin on Long Lake. I spent a few days there just recuperating.

The year was 1939. My search for employment was still in progress. I answered an ad in Field & Stream magazine and got a job working at a northern fur farm in Sharon, Massachusetts, a little town 20 miles south of Boston. My job was to prepare the feed for 45 silver foxes and 650 minks, and then go around and feed them all. It was summer time and when it wasn't drizzling, it was pouring. The humidity was terrible. I worked there for a couple of months and quit.

Now, World War II was upon us. Wartime was hard times for jobs, but my Dad had a connection at U.S. Aluminum in Cleveland, which landed me a job at the unheard of wage of $1.30 an hour. It was in the forge division where they pound out crankcases and other parts for war planes. The forge shop was next to the shipping department and most of the shipments were going to Japan. Ironically, a couple of years later, Japan used these very parts against us at Pearl Harbor.

In 1940, while I was working at U.S. Aluminum, they started drafting men for the army. I didn't want to be a foot soldier, so I applied for the Air Force. I figured I might as well be a pilot and learn something. I always wanted to be a fighter pilot. I was rejected because of my respiratory problems. Maybe it was a good thing. All of my buddies at that time went into the Air Force…none of them came back…not one.

I continued to work at my job there in Cleveland. Grand Rapids, Michigan was the hometown of a buddy of mine from work. Donald Engler invited me to drive home with him one weekend to visit friends and family. He introduced me to his sister, Bea. That became the beginning of a weekend ritual that only the intensity of youth could perform week after week. We left our swing shift at twelve o'clock midnight on Friday driving 6 or 7 hours non-stop for Grand Rapids. We'd spend time there with my buddy's girlfriend and Bea, and without sleeping, we'd drive back to Cleveland, go to work and never hit the pillow until Monday night.

After one Friday shift on a particularly cold and miserable night, nobody in the parking lot at the plant could even start their car to get home. Determined to get on our way to Michigan, I had to come up with some inspiration to get that '29 Model "A" Ford going. At the risk of having Ford turn over in his grave, my idea worked. I "p"ed on the carburetor. It started right up and we were on the road.

In 1940, I married Beatrice Engler who, thankfully by now had moved to Cleveland. I continued to work at U.S. Aluminum. A year later, my first son, Bobby, was born. We lived in a 19-foot trailer about four miles from the U.S. Aluminum plant. We could hear the drop forges that far away. No wonder my ears are bad today. I continued to work, but I kept my interest in photography and shot pictures whenever I could. I won a national contest with a picture of Bobby wearing a big straw hat sitting on an old wood fence.

By 1943, I had paid for the trailer and a brand new Buick convertible. In October, we headed for Florida. The new Buick broke down in Gainesville, Florida. I took it to Melton Motors, the local Buick dealer. They said it would take a week to make the repairs, and being short on funds, I had to work on a farm feeding pigs and cutting pine trees with a crosscut saw to pay for the repairs. When I picked up the car a week later, the mechanical problem was no better, but the dealer refused to make the necessary repairs to get the engine to run properly. My warranty was supposed to take care of it. There was a hole in the top of a piston, but he simply wouldn't fix it. I presumed it to be the south's hatred of people from the north.

I drove the Buick, which was barely running, and pulled the trailer to my old hangout in South Florida where I met up with a friend I knew from Ohio. He was a carpenter and told me that carpenters were scarce during wartime and that he could probably get me a job. I told him I knew nothing about carpenter work. He still insisted on taking me down to the union hall to

Butchering horses for a fur farm in Sharon, MA 20 miles south of Boston. I am taking the picture. I had the job of mixing the food for 45 Silver Foxes and 600 Minks. It rained for two months, so I went back to Cleveland.

I went to work in my Model "A" Ford

Bobby Jr. at the piano

Bobby Jr. in the snow

Bobby Jr. with his paddle and canoe

Trailer life in a
Cleveland trailer park
Me, Bea and little Bobby

apply for a union card. I missed every question on the test, but they made me a journeyman carpenter anyway. Normally, they required at least three years apprenticeship before you could get a journeyman's card. So, off I went to work with my friend who helped me in this difficult job market. The foreman of the job knew I was inexperienced, but Roy told him he would quit if I was fired. Heck, I didn't even know how to read a level or which way the bubble was supposed to go. But by the end of that winter, I could do any kind of carpenter job including cabinetry work and hanging doors.

As part of the construction crew, we completed the first building at the University of Miami at Coral Gables, from the foundation to the final touch of hanging the doors. When this was done, I decided to head west with my family. I had traded the Buick in for an old 1935 Ford truck. We backed it up to the trailer and headed west to Arizona. Still struggling with my allergies, everyone advised me that Tucson was the best place to go for respiratory problems, so that's where we set our destination. I was there one day and one night; my allergies were so bad I thought I was going to die. If my wife, Bea, hadn't driven me out of there, I probably *would* have died. By the time we got to the mountains in Prescott, Arizona, my allergies had completely disappeared. I spent a couple of months building houses in Prescott and enjoyed the cool weather and beautiful pine country. Every weekend we would take the old truck and head in a different direction. On one of these trips we drove over Mingus Mountain and came into Sedona from the west. The scenery was unbelievable; we had a wonderful day. After wrapping things up in Prescott, we moved on to Flagstaff and I got a job building a motel. Our little trailer home was parked at Lindberg Spring, eight miles south of Flagstaff.

While I was away working one day, a tragedy nearly besieged our family. My wife, Bea, had fallen asleep and little Bobby, then four years old, almost drowned in the spring near our home. By chance, a tourist happened to come along and pull him out just in time. Only God's hand could have prevented this. We were grateful that he was saved and we kept a keen eye on him after that.

During that summer in Flagstaff, it frequently rained all afternoon stopping the construction work on site. So, with work called off, Bea, Bobby and I got in the old truck and headed for Sedona. The gentle, mild rain and the seductive landscape made us fall in love with Sedona. We were sure we wanted to live in this paradise that had captured our hearts. My job in Flagstaff was over in November and I worked on tract houses on a Dell Webb development in Phoenix. Once again, the climate didn't suit us, so we went to San Diego. San Diego had been said to have the most even climate anywhere. By the time we left San Diego, we said "Yeah, 'even' worse than anywhere else". I got a job building an apartment house and we stayed in a trailer park near the job site. In those years, the climate in San Diego was very cold. Getting up early for work, I had my go-to-work morning routine; after my cup of hot coffee, I took a pot of hot water to pour on the windshield to melt the ice. I couldn't stand the weather, so we headed for Los Angeles. L.A. was worse for us than San Diego. We didn't want any part of that city rat race. While we were there, we parked overnight in a trailer camp in Azusa. That night was the worst damp, chilling climate I have ever experienced. I remember that the water in the sink inside of the trailer froze during the night because the window over the sink was open just one inch.

Needless to say, we were on our way again and ended up on the desert at Cathedral City about 5 miles out of Palm Springs, California. It was just a wide place in the road back then, but there was a good trailer park to stay in. We loved the climate there, between December and March it was terrific, so we decided to settle in for a while. Still, we did have some hard times

Bobby followed me around while I
took photographs of the wonderous
terrain. He would often become
part of the photo shoot.
Bea went with us too, and the
result was a collection of photos
that are now part of the
Bradshaw archives.

Bob Bradshaw Autobiography

Bobby Jr. on Ira Piper's colt — I'm riding Ira's horse.

This is the way the Chapel area looked when we lived there.

There were only the Pipers and the Bradshaws in Little Horse Park.

there. It was a union town and no contractor would hire you unless the union hall sent you out. The man at the union hall was sending his friends out to the jobs, hoping we would move on to some other place. The man next to me in the trailer park was from Oklahoma and he was in the same boat. Neither of us had any money to move on even if we wanted to. We were having a hard time keeping bread on the table. Fortunately, the man who owned the trailer park liked kids and he let us stay there until we could get a job and pay him. Through a stroke of good luck and a lot of prayers, I met a man who had a cabinet shop who wasn't with the union. He was willing to hire me to install cabinets in the high-end houses of his clientele. Homes being built for celebrities like Frank Sinatra, Hedy Lamarr and Marjorie Main were among the houses I helped to build.

Finally, the business agent at the union hall got a call for two men to go to La Quinta. La Quinta was so far away his friends didn't want the job, so he gave it to me and the man from Oklahoma. It was just the ticket for us. It was a $100,000 ranch house, which at that time was expensive. It was the home of Walter Kirchner who owned the Greyson Robinson dress stores. We worked there from beginning to end, from the foundation to the finish work. Can you imagine what this $100,000 house would cost today?

In my spare time, I built a little camper for the truck. In that time period, campers didn't exist. I fixed it up with a water tank, beds, kitchen and everything. If I had been a bit more entrepreneurial, I would have gotten a patent on it and made my fortune.

Around the first of April, Palm Springs and Cathedral City turned into a 130-degree inferno and the wind blew sand into everything. So, we moved north to Riverside where I got a job on an assembly line subdivision. The heat and the humidity were unbearable and the amount of work they expected you to do was impossible. They put the material for the walls and partitions on the lot. Then they expected two men to put up all the walls and partitions on a big house and garage in one day. This included doubling up the plates on the walls. If you got the roof detail, they expected two men to put up all the rafters over the house and garage, put in all the braces and freeze blocks. It was just too much to expect, especially with the hot weather. But if a worker couldn't handle it, there would be other carpenters waiting for the job. So, we sold the little trailer that had been our home for so long and, once again, headed out for the Northwest. Before I left, I bought a 4x5 Crown Graphic camera in Palm Springs. It was a great camera delivering wonderful shots, which recorded that era of my life quite effectively.

On July 4th, we visited my sister Holly in Seattle. It was so cold we asked her to put on the heat. She just laughed at us and said it was a nice warm day. We asked about Mt. Rainier and she said they very rarely saw it because the weather was usually cloudy. We didn't like the Northwest at all, so we headed back down the eastern slopes of the Sierra Nevada Mountains and found the only area in California, Bishop and Lone Pine, that we really liked. But because there was no work there, we headed back to Arizona.

When we got to Prescott, we didn't know whether to head east to Florida or go back to Sedona. Those were our favorite places. We decided that if we could sell the graphic camera, we would go to Florida and if we couldn't, we would go to Sedona. The guy in the camera store didn't want the 4x5, so we didn't go to Florida. Little did he know how much he was influencing my future by his actions. The camera, which I used for so many amazing photographs stayed, and so did we to capture the scenic wonder of our pristine surroundings.

Trailer on the road
leaving Michigan

University of Florida at Coral Gables, Florida

Walter Kirschner's House in La Quinta

I spent months building the camper.

I took this shot of Yosemite.

My old truck and my camper at the redwoods

12 feet of snow – Lassen Park

My camper on the road

Luck was with us again when I ran into a contractor, Mr. Ragle, on the street in Prescott. He offered me a job in Cottonwood. We needed a place in the shade for our camper truck, but Cottonwood didn't have an appropriate location for us, so we explored the possibilities in Sedona. The hands of fate brought us to what I will always consider the Paradise of the United States. I have yet to have anyone prove to me that there is a better year-round climate than Sedona. Merle Crawford let me keep the camper in the shade of some giant Cottonwood trees on his peaceful land just below the bridge in Morgan's Draw. Today, Merle's old house is still there and the rest of the land is a trailer park. I got a job building the Sedona Lodge just up the road. I was down to 3 cents in my pocket before I got my first paycheck.

Sedona Lodge, my construction site, was built to accommodate motion picture companies that wanted to film the scenery of Oak Creek canyon. Before Sedona Lodge was built, companies had to stay at the Weatherford or Monte Vista Hotel in Flagstaff and commute to Sedona.

After some time on the job and with as much money saved as possible and still keep ourselves going, I built a small farmhouse out of lumber from the mill at Flagstaff. You could take a ton and a half truck to the mill and they would load it with clean, straight dry lumber. The cost was $25 a load for #1 pine or $10 to $15 a load for other grades. We picked out a spot to build the house on what is known as Little Horse Park (it's now called the Chapel area, but the chapel hadn't been built yet). Lee Piper, another early resident of the area, owned that land. We bought four acres from Lee for $400. He traded 17 acres to Speed Wilson for a beat up Dodge Truck.

The Lee Piper family and the Bradshaw family were the only people in that area for a long time. Our son, Bobby, and their two kids went to school together. When they got off the bus, the Piper kids would pick on Bobby. So my wife, Bea, waited for them on the road and knocked their heads together. That stopped the entire hassle with the Piper kids.

By the end of summer of 1947, we were a lot better off financially. My skills for building and my abilities with horses and cattle along with my knowledge of the entire region made me a valuable asset in the making of the many motion pictures here in the Red Rock Country. It was a source of income for me for over 50 years and remains a source of income for me still today. I was part of the crew that built the original set under Coffee Pot Rock, which was used for many movies until it was torn down in 1960.

Throughout this time, I continued to shoot scenic photographs of the region. Bobby was just a youngster. He'd follow me around while I took photographs of our wondrous terrain. Often he would become part of the photo shoot. Bea went with us, too, and the result was a collection of photos that are now part of the Bradshaw archives.

In October of 1947, I had a chance to go to Monument Valley to work as a carpenter on a fort being built for John Ford's movie, *She Wore a Yellow Ribbon* starring John Wayne. This film is now considered John Wayne's best. I left the truck with Bea because Little Horse Park was too far from town to walk. When I got back, the truck was gone. Bea told me that when I sent the first paycheck from Monument Valley, she went down to the store and paid Glen Blanton the $45.00 grocery bill we owed. She trusted the grocer and didn't get a receipt. The grocer claimed he was never paid and went to our place and took the truck to cover the bill. With the Sheriff's help, we got the truck back, but the little crook took us to court and with no evidence of payment, the court ruled against us. I'm sure Bea was telling the truth, so we ended up paying the bill twice.

Sedona Lodge

The Sedona Lodge was built in 1946 to accommodate motion picture companies that normally would have to stay in Flagstaff to work in Sedona. It was torn down in 1964 and replaced by King's Ransom Quality Inn.

As more movie production developed in the area, I gravitated to every movie I got wind of. When *She Wore a Yellow Ribbon* was slated for filming, I wanted to get cast as a cavalry soldier. Bea, Bobby and I drove to Monument Valley where we were told that the Mormon Bishop in Blanding, Utah was hiring the soldiers. So, we drove all night on a terrible road to get there. I remember our gas line kept clogging up and every few miles I had to get out of the truck and blow it out. In the morning, we went to see the Bishop who matter of factly said he was hiring only Mormon people. We explained our situation to this man of God, but it didn't matter to him that we were broke and didn't have enough money for gas to get home to Sedona. The road from Monument Valley heading back to Flagstaff was all dirt. One section of the road was like a roller coaster dipping up and down so much you couldn't tell if another car was coming. Suddenly, a big limousine appeared at the top of a dip. We must have scared the driver who slammed on the brakes. As we passed them, to our surprise, we watched Duke Wayne flying to the floor.

Having just enough gas to get to Flagstaff, we went to the motion picture office at the Monte Vista Hotel to try to get hired. Fortunately, Lee Doyle, who handled transportation, supplied livestock and assisted in gathering up the wranglers was a friend of mine. This helped me get a job as a wrangler. Bea went back to Sedona and I went with Lee Doyle and the rest of the wranglers back up to Monument Valley. The company was now ready to shoot. On one hand, the caterer, Anderson Dunham, prepared the best food anyone ever ate. On the other hand, the tent they set up was the most miserable place I ever lived in. It was November at 7,000 feet altitude and the big tents had only one little stove to keep us warm at night. While we piled blankets as high as a tall Indian's ass, we remained chilled to the bone. Lee Doyle and I took turns standing directly on top of the stove trying to keep warm through the night. The film stars had the only decent place to stay, which was up at Goulding's Lodge. I remember one night the Navajo's had a squaw dance. At a squaw dance, they dance around the fire all night. At intervals, they would stop and relax. During this time, there was dead silence. Most of the actors were gathered around watching this colorful ceremony with the fire blazing against the dark starlit sky. I remember John Wayne, Joanne Dru, Victor McLaglen and John Agar being completely mesmerized by this ancient Indian ritual. During the lull, John Agar said to a young Navajo boy next to him, "I really admire your people for living out here in this wilderness and putting up with all of the hardships you endure." The Navajo boy just looked at him and said nothing. Then John Agar asked him, "What part of the reservation are you from?" The crowd around the fire was listening intently. The Navajo boy answered "Riverside, California." Everybody burst into laughter.

We finished the film and headed back towards Flagstaff. On the way, we stopped at Grey Mountain, which was the first trading post off the reservation about 35 miles north of Flagstaff. Back in those days if anyone wanted to buy liquor, they had to drive 150 miles to Grey Mountain. Liquor was not allowed on the reservation. All the wranglers were in the crowded trading post, which was full of tourists. John Wayne and director, John Ford were pushing their way through. The Duke went over to the counter where the native crafted Kachina Dolls filled the shelves on the back wall. He stacked his arms full of these colorful, hand carved Hopi dolls made from cottonwood trees, paid for them, and then climbed back into the limousine headed for Flagstaff. Like wildfire, word got around that the cowboy boots of The Duke were kicking up dust in our territory. People were rubbing shoulders with him in the crowd completely unaware. After they heard he was there, they were all trying to find him to take pictures and get a look at him. By that time, he was well on his way to Flagstaff and heading back to Hollywood.

1948 *She Wore a Yellow Ribbon*

John Wayne stands on the right talking to the production manager during a break on location for
She wore a Yellow Ribbon. Actors eat their lunch at the table with Monument Valley in the background.

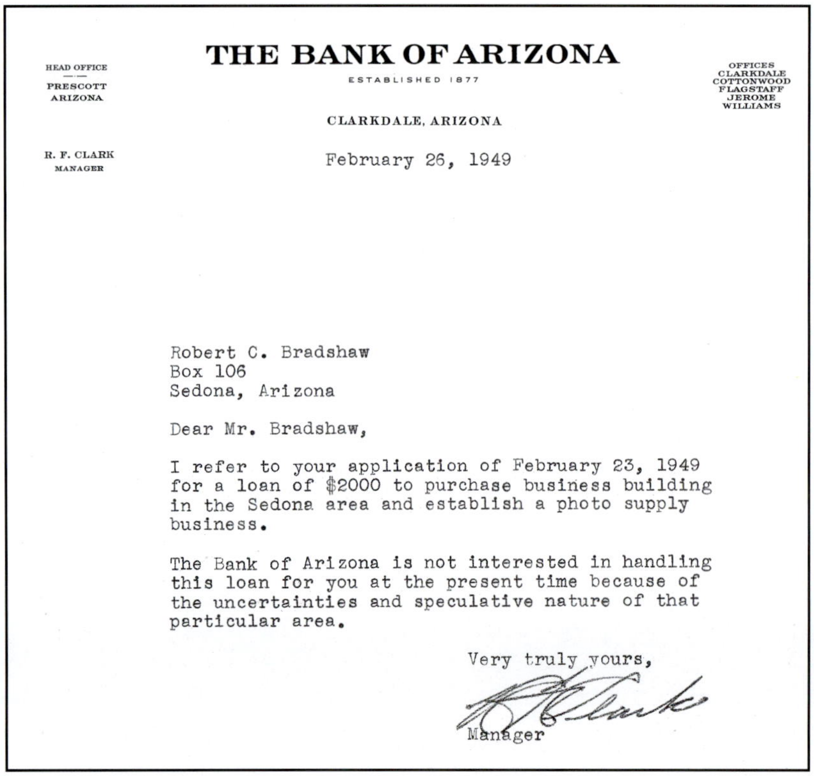

THE BANK OF ARIZONA

ESTABLISHED 1877

HEAD OFFICE
———
PRESCOTT
ARIZONA

OFFICES
CLARKDALE
COTTONWOOD
FLAGSTAFF
JEROME
WILLIAMS

R. F. CLARK
MANAGER

CLARKDALE, ARIZONA

February 26, 1949

Robert C. Bradshaw
Box 106
Sedona, Arizona

Dear Mr. Bradshaw,

I refer to your application of February 23, 1949
for a loan of $2000 to purchase business building
in the Sedona area and establish a photo supply
business.

The Bank of Arizona is not interested in handling
this loan for you at the present time because of
the uncertainties and speculative nature of that
particular area.

Very truly yours,

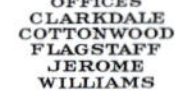

Manager

In 1949, I got the idea that a camera shop would be a good business in the picturesque setting of Sedona. The bank manager of the Clarkdale Branch of the Bank of Arizona, Mr. R.F. Clark, didn't seem to think Sedona was a good risk. Today, of course, Sedona is one of the most photographed areas in the world.

As for me, I was happy to be heading home too. I will never forget the beautiful warm climate of Sedona compared to the raw cold of Monument Valley. Even the Sedona nights were warm and as I drove homeward, the full moon came up between the buttes on the horizon, which made for an incredible sight.

In January of '48, we got a lot of snow. Elsworth Viergge bought two acres next to us and had put up a tent before the snows came. It piled up to 30 inches and Elsworth was still in his tent. Wish I had pictures of that. Flagstaff got 120 inches that January and everything was at a stand-still. There was no work in Sedona, so I went to the carpenters' union hall in Flagstaff to see if there was some inside work. There was just enough room on Hwy. 89A for two cars to pass with the snow piled 20 feet high on each side. When I got to the alley where the union hall was, they told me there was no work of any kind. If things weren't already bad enough, as I was walking down the alley to my car, some guy shoveling snow off the roof threw a big shovel full right onto my head. You might say I was down and out in Flagstaff. So, it was back to Sedona and two weeks digging my truck out of the mud and snow. I carried Bobby to the school bus because the snow was too deep for him to walk through. Our generous grocer, Burt Blem, grubstaked a lot of us or we would have starved to death. Elsworth took to the woods trying to kill a rabbit or a deer to help us survive. The snow was still two feet deep around his tent.

In the spring of '49, I had an idea. There was no place in Sedona to buy a roll of color film. Downtown across the road from Burt Blem's store was a small cinder block building with a sign. POP MILLER'S POPCORN, building for $1200, including the land. I got busy and started to talk to the banks, and it seemed I had everything in place to buy this spot. Then the bank in Clarkdale threw me a curve and wouldn't loan me the money. Pop Miller wanted out anyway, so he said he would rent it to me for $15 a month. So, I started up a little store with the supplies I bought from the camera store in Flagstaff. Every time I had to replenish my stock, I would take the bus up to Flag, an hours drive one way, at the cost of fifty cents for a round trip ticket.

After Jean & Trox Camera Shop took their profit, I couldn't make enough for myself. So I started writing to Ansco Color and Kodak West Coast Distributors to see if I could buy direct from them. I explained the potential of a camera store in Sedona (because of the scenery). They wrote back letters, which suggested that I was crazy to even ask for a dealership in a wide place in the road like Sedona. One day when I was in town, I saw Jack Fry. He was not only President of TWA Airlines but President of Ansco Color, too. While flying over the area one day, his wife fell in love with the red rocks. He had just purchased 800 acres on lower Oak Creek for his wife, Helen. I told him about my problems with the Ansco L.A. office. He told me not to worry, that he would take care of it for me. A couple of days later, three guys from the L.A office in their fancy suits were standing in the doorway of my little store asking, "What can we do for you". With this advantage, I then wrote to Mr. McGee, the Vice President of Kodak, and he set me up with a Kodak Dealership. This little store that I started in 1949 is making more money today on film than any store in Arizona. Now I wonder who was crazy.

That summer, lightening hit the little house I built and burned it to the ground. Lee Piper said he saw the lightening hit twice. Lee was known for stretching the truth a lot. He used to sit up at his house and read adventure stories and then go downtown to the store and tell the same stories to the tourists as if it had happened to him. One day he would be a Canadian Northwest Mounted Policeman. The next day, he would be a Ranger on the Border Patrol or an ace with a World War I fighter plane. My wife told him one day "You know, Lee, if you did all those things you say you did, you would be as old as Methuselah." Lee Piper answered, "You know, I used to know Methuselah."

This temporary store was built next to the Hitching Post. The foundation and the stone wall were planned to be a part of the finished building. The slab fence was put there to keep tourists from falling into the foundation.

I built the walls of the store around the temporary building. The photo shop remained open during the construction.

Me on my Palomino at the big red rock next to Coffee Pot Rock leading a party of riders. We passed this rock every day. It is also in the center of the photo below.

Bob Bradshaw Autobiography

I drew this sketch of the layout of the finished store.

Back in 1945, George Brolley built the Hitching Post Restaurant – that is a story in itself.

The finished store with poles set up to build a photo tower. We built a corral behind the store and rented horses for trail rides.

This is the tempory slab fence built on the foundation wall to keep tourists from falling into the space for building the floor joists.

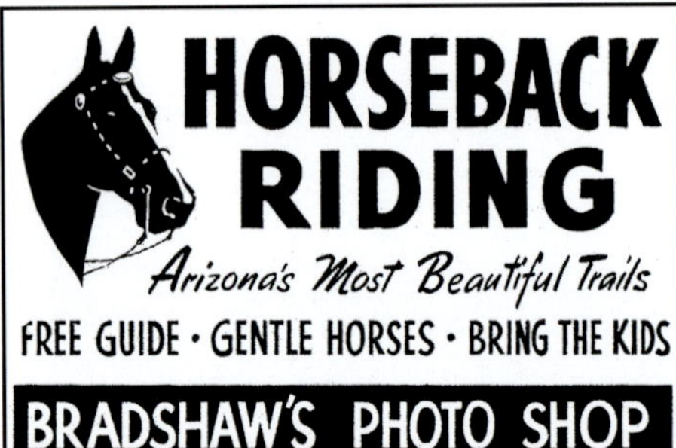

I finally built a house behind the camera shop.

Riders on Bradshaw Trail when I took people out on scenic horseback rides.

Back in those days, we made a lot of pictures where Lee and I lived. There was a big set in the middle of Little Horse Park that was used for *Angel and the Badman* (John Wayne), *Blood on the Moon* (Robert Mitchum) and *Desert Fury* (Elizabeth Scott, Burt Lancaster, & John Hodiak). They not only used the set, but they also made use of the beautiful scenery. More movies shot in that location were *Eagle and the Hawk* (John Payne), *Drum Beat* (Alan Ladd). *Gun Fury* (Rock Hudson, Donna Reed), *Outlaw's Daughter* (Bill Williams, Kelly Ryan, Jim Davis), *Dallas* (Josh Ewing), *Johnny Guitar* (Sterling Hayden, Joan Crawford), *Indian Uprising* (George Montgomery, Audrey Long) and *Cheyenne* (Dennis Morgan, Jane Wyman). When Piper saw a film production start up, he would get out his tractor and make a lot of dust in the background so the film people would have to pay him to stop his work. It seemed that was the only time he'd do any work with his tractor.

In 1949, we made a picture in Sedona called *Broken Arrow* starring James Stewart, Jeff Chandler and Debra Paget. I worked as a carpenter while Bea ran our little photo supply store. The Hollywood carpenter boss, Paul Wurtzel, liked me a lot and gave me several truckloads of lumber that were left over from the set construction. I transported them over to the four acres I bought in Little Horse Park up by where the Chapel is now. We got all the plaster of Paris saguaros from the set and put them in front of the camera store. Later that year, a man from Montana bought our little store from Pop Miller and informed me that the rent would be $35 a month instead of $15. I told him to shove it.

Back in 1945, George Brolley built the Hitching Post Restaurant. A couple of years later, he built the Hitching Post Motel. He was interested in selling curios and I wanted to build a photo shop, so I suggested that he buy the land and I would build the store. He said it sounded like a good idea. When he went back to Chicago that winter, he said he would keep in touch with me and we would make plans. Well, I never heard from Brolley, so I went down to see Elsie Riordan and she sold me the land for $35 per month. Being a carpenter myself, I took the lumber we got from the *Broken Arrow* set and built a temporary store on site while the final structure of the camera shop was being constructed. That camera shop still sits proudly in uptown today.

When Brolley came back in the spring, he had the top down on his Cadillac convertible and was headed down the highway to make a deal with Elsie. I was standing in the doorway of my little shop and he was smoking his cigar, not bothering to even look my way. When he found out I had already bought the land, he was madder than hell. The first thing he did was go down the street where Oaxaca Restaurant is now and bought that land. He figured if he could get ahead of me on the highway he could sell all the film and run me out of business. The land he bought happened to be a big gully, so he got some carryalls and took the top off the hill where the Matterhorn Motel now stands and filled up the canyon. Then he built the store on top of the hill (now Oaxaca). He discovered that the tourists wouldn't drive up the slope to the store, so he got the carryalls back and dug it out to its present level. All of this effort to get ahead of me and try to put me out of business. He even built a photo tower and put FILM on it in big letters. This didn't stop as many people as he thought it would either, so he changed the position of it three times in an attempt to maximize his position. In spite of everything he tried, I kept getting more and more business until the little store I built from Fox Films set materials on *Broken Arrow* turned into a big fancy store.

Most of the lumber Fox gave me was 2x12's; even the sheathing boards on the roof are 2x12. The store hasn't sagged an eighth of an inch in 50 years. I not only sold a lot of film, but I started publishing post cards of Northern Arizona and as of the year 2000, I will have been in the

1946 *Angel and the Badman* - John Wayne and Gail Russel

1948 *Blood on the Moon* - Robert Mitchum and
Barbara Bel Gaddes

1947 *Desert Fury* - Burt Lancaster, Lizbeth Scott
and John Hodiak

1950 *Eagle and the Hawk* - John Payne, Rhonda Fleming
and Dennis O'Keefe

1954 *Drum Beat*

1954 *Drum Beat* - Alan Ladd

1952 *Flaming Feather* -
Montezuma Castle was used as a location

1947 *Cheyenne* - Dennis Morgan and Jane Wyman

1959 *Yellowstone Kelly Cavalry* -
starring Clint Walker on the run

1949 *Broken Arrow* - James Stewart pinned
to a tree with arrows

1949 *Broken Arrow* - starring Jeff Chandler,
James Stewart and Debra Paget

scenic card business for 50 years. We also started the first trail ride for tourists in uptown Sedona. The corral was right behind the store. I guess you'd have to say I was the one who started the tour business before the jeep companies went into business. Now my youngest sons are carrying on with their jeep tour and horseback ride company, A Day In The West, taking people to Bradshaw Ranch where the old movie sets still exist standing against time...just like me. I decided to use my photographs to print postcards for tourists to buy send home. My son, John, now owns and runs that business today.

Besides the postcard business, I realized there was another need that I could fill by using my photographic skills. Tourist businesses were being developed and they needed promotional materials. The first commercial brochure job I photographed was an exterior and interior for a Dude Ranch called the **Mystery Ranch** where **Back O' Beyond** is now. Still today, I make cards and brochures for local businesses, some of which I've done business with for over a half century. I'd say that's pretty rare today in any business.

That year, 1950, a shot of the buggy we used to drive around town was used for our Christmas card. I posed for this photo to help advertise our Sheriff's Posse organization. It was called the Oak Creek Rifles of which I was a charter member. There was not much profit in renting horses, but it was fun seeing all of the trails within 10 miles of Sedona. The insurance for riding was not expensive in those days.

One winter we set up horseback rides at Arizona Manor, a resort in Phoenix on 24th Street and Camelback Road. From there, we crossed 24th Street and used the Biltmore Trails all the way to Squaw Peak. At that time, the resort catered to Hollywood stars. Joanne Dru and John Ireland and their kids would come for a week at a time. They rode with me every day of their stay. I shot pictures of the family the last time they rode. They turned out great and I wanted to get the photos to them, but I doubted they'd get them if I sent them to their agent, so I just hung on to them.

One day many years later, I was in the trading post in Cottonwood buying a John Wayne Poster. When the shop owner was in the process of wrapping it, I mentioned that I worked on John Wayne films. He asked if I worked on *She Wore a Yellow Ribbon*. I said I did. He questioned me, "Well, who was the girl in that movie?" I replied, "Joanne Dru." "That's right...she's is my sister!" We shook hands and later I brought in those photographs for him to send to his sister. It took fifty years for those kids to see themselves on the trail. I understand Joanne passed into movie heaven shortly after that.

Well, we about broke even on this Phoenix venture until we loaded up the horses on the 1935 one-ton Ford Truck. The weather was perfect to head home. The I-17 freeway didn't exist yet. The only way you could get to Sedona was through Wickenburg and up Yarnell Hill to Prescott. We had seven horses aboard. Halfway up Yarnell Hill, the rod bearings burned out and we had to be towed to a corral at the top of the hill. The man in the garage said he would have the truck ready in two days. Two weeks later, the truck was ready and there was a blizzard blowing in Yarnell. The horses had no winter hair because of the warm winter in Phoenix and they were shivering from the cold wind and snow. I loaded them up in the blizzard and started up the road to Prescott. In the mountains near Prescott, the storm got worse and the windshield wipers were not working, so I had to hold my head out of the window just to see where I was going. Bea and Bobby had gone back to Sedona so *they* were all right, but I sure wasn't doing so well. When I got to Prescott, the storm broke and I crossed Lonesome Valley to the bottom of Mingus

Top: In 1949, Sedona looked like this. The little building at the end of row was my little store.

Middle: Bea and I posed in front of our shop.

Bottom: What is now uptown was all of Sedona's commercial area. Steamboat and Wilson Mountain are in the background.

Mystery Ranch - My first advertising job at Back O' Beyond.

     Bob Bradshaw Autobiography

This magnificent photograph, taken in Oak Creek canyon, was sweepstakes winner in the amateur photograph contest conducted by Jean & Trox. The original is in natural color. It was made by R. B. Bradshaw, a carpenter, at Sedona. He develops his own color pictures. (Black and white negative by Griff Morris of the DAILY SUN Staff.)

Eddie Ellinger's Dude Ranch
My first commercial job with postcards. No houses in sight in all of West Sedona.

Top: Bea with wagon wheel at store

Left: Bobby Jr. acting up with an arrow

Bottom: My first photograph accepted in *Arizona Highways Magazine*. They used my photographs from 1950 through 1985.

Top - Bobby Jr. on Paint horse at Tlaquepaque where we used the pasture before anyone built there. We kept our horses there for five years.

Bottom - Art Barn

Charlie Brewer and his cows going north on what is now 179A.

Ellsworth Verrige, Ira Smith and Earl Van Deren branding in Uptown
Sedona across from the present day Chamber of Commerce.

Bobby Jr. on Blue Roan

Bob Bradshaw Autobiography

Mayhew's Lodge

Oak Creek Canyon - Indian Gardens store and Roller Rink with Wilson Mountain in the background

Oak Creek at Junipine

Snow scene up the canyon

Pendley's Barn burned down many years ago.

Purtyman cabin

Original bridge at Indian Gardens

Chavez Homestead

Lo Lomai Lodge - Where Zane Grey wrote *Call of the Canyon* near West Fork

Mountain. It was late in the day and it was bitter cold. I got halfway up the mountain and the same bearings that were supposed to be fixed went out again. Now I was stranded with the seven horses. Fortunately, they were not cold because they were crammed together in the truck. I was pretty lucky because a snowplow came along and towed me to the top of the mountain. They dropped me off at the Mingus Mountain Inn. The snow was 6 feet deep and I had no way to get home with the horses. I considered jumping them out and trailing them to Sedona or calling for a tow. Tony's garage in Jerome had a night phone and he sent his truck up to pull me home. Most of it was down hill except for one place halfway down the mountain. It was steep and icy. Tony's wife was driving and she was moving inch by inch. By this time, it was about 3 a.m. and the temperature must have been zero. I couldn't run the heater and I was wet from the snow. After what seemed like an eternity, we finally made it to Sedona. I had the tow truck push me back into a cinder pile in the middle of town so the horses could get down from the truck. I pulled down the tailgate and let the horses out, running free after such a long and difficult journey. The stove and the warm bed at home never felt better in my life. In the morning before sunrise, I set out to track the horses. The trail in the 15 inch snow led me to the Walter Jordan Ranch. The fruit trees had already blossomed and so, to protect the crop, Walter had fire pots flaming under all of his trees to keep them from freezing. This sight made a fantastic scene in the snow that I would have given anything to have been able to photograph.

After 5 years of trail riding with the public, we gave it up because our other businesses were taking precedence. In the meantime, I was still working on the movies. I helped build the set for *Copper Canyon* at Red Rock Crossing. It was filmed right after *Broken Arrow*. The stars in that production were Ray Milland and Hedy Lamar. Each night, Milland would walk by our store headed for the bar with a blonde on each arm. I asked him one day how he liked Sedona; he told me he liked it a lot. Then I asked him if he would like to live in Sedona and he said, "I would rather sit on my front porch in L.A. and watch the traffic go by."

In 1951, I worked as a carpenter on the movie *Red Head and The Cowboy* starring Glenn Ford, Rhonda Fleming and Edmond O'Brien. We built a barn on the Woo Ranch and fixed up the old frame house with gun ports and shuttered windows. Since then, the frame house burned down and they built one out of concrete blocks, which stands today.

I worked on *Half-Breed* in 1952 as an actor in the cavalry. On the same movie, I also got the job as both a double and a stand-in for Robert Young. By way of explanation, certain job titles often get confused in filmmaking. A "double" is an actor who is actually filmed as the star and is in the final cut of the movie. They are costumed exactly like the star in each scene and are usually in a long shot where it's hard to see the face very well. For instance, I did a lot of horseback riding for stars when it was too dangerous or when they were just not skilled enough to ride. A "stand-in", on the other hand, does just that. They stand in the place on the set where the star will actually be while they are setting up the lighting and preparing the scene. The star can be off set using his time more effectively until they start "rolling film". In both cases, the actor has to have a close physical resemblance to the star. An "extra", which is often confused with a "double" or "stand-in", is a very different job. "Extras", or "atmosphere actors", are the background in a scene, sometimes hardly seen on camera but necessary to make a scene work.

That same year I worked on *Flaming Feather*, starring Sterling Hayden, Barbara Rush and Victor Jory. We built a set at Montezuma Castle on the cliff above the rim to represent the inside of the ruin for the fight scenes. The view below was the same as if it was filmed in the castle itself. We also changed the park service ladders to Indian ladders, which was a big job. In 1953,

Copper Canyon set at Red Rock Crossing

1951 *Indian Uprising* - George Montgomery

1953 *Gun Fury* - I doubled Lee Marvin and Rock Hudson

1953 *Gun Fury* - Rock Hudson and Donna Reed

Sterling Hayden and
Yvonne de Carlo riding
Hayden's Buckskin
through the set in
Little Horse Park
Sedona, now called
the Chapel area.

These open plains
are now filled
with houses.

Bob Bradshaw Autobiography

I worked on *Gun Fury* and doubled Rock Hudson, Lee Marvin and a Mexican actor. *Johnny Guitar* was also made that year and I rode through most of the picture with Ward Bond. We were the men in black suits that he rounded up out of the funeral scene to chase Scott Brady, Ernest Borgnine and the rest of the bad men. Sterling Hayden, Joan Crawford and Mercedes McCambridge were the stars. When I was a kid listening to *I Love a Mystery* on the radio, I never dreamed I would be working with the star of that radio show, Mercedes McCambridge. She was very pleasant and easy to work with and well liked by the cast and crew.

In 1954, I worked on *Apache* as a mounted Indian scout. Charles Bronson was our leader in this script. His name was Charles Buchinsky then. Burt Lancaster and Jean Peters starred in the film. That same year, I worked on "Drumbeat" as a cavalry soldier. Warner Brothers changed Buchinsky's name to Bronson and he played opposite Alan Ladd in his first big role. I worked as a stand-in and double for Zachary Scott on "Shotgun" in 1955. The other stars were Sterling Hayden and Yvonne De Carlo. That same year I worked on a picture called *Stranger on Horseback* with Joel McCrea and John McIntyre.

In 1956, I worked on the *Last Wagon* as a double for Timothy Carey who was one of the bad-men chasing Richard Widmark. I worked as an extra in "3:10 to Yuma" in 1957 starring Glenn Ford, Van Heflin and Felicia Farr. Right after that in the same year, I worked on *Yellowstone Kelly* as a cavalry soldier. We started the picture in Flagstaff with 165 soldiers and they sent about 20 of us to Sedona to have a war with the Indians. Clint Walker and John Russell were the stars.

Besides working on screen, I took advantage of all of my western skills and knowledge of the region whenever I could. Production jobs behind the scenes held a lot of potential for good people. There was a guy around Sedona in the 40's and 50's who was handling the location work like I do now, but he got a little greedy and the movie companies didn't like it. He would contract horses from the ranchers for $3.00 a day and then charge the picture companies $5.00. He was paid for the job position, and wasn't expected to take another cut for himself. Producers didn't like this. If a horse was $3.00 a day, that's what they wanted to pay. The ranchers weren't too happy about it when they found out either. If the company was paying $5.00, that's what they wanted to be paid. Opportunity opened up for me through someone else's poor judgment.

My first job as coordinator, or contact man as they called us back then, was in 1956, securing the wagons and horses for the *Twenty Six Men* television series. I also worked as one of the 26 Arizona Rangers and did some of the stunts. I have been contact man, coordinator, location manager, production manager, wrangler and actor ever since I sold the camera store in the early 60's and bought a 130-acre ranch in the beautiful valley of the Red Canyon area.

1954 *The Outlaws Daughter* - Bill Williams and Kelly Ryan

1955 *Shotgun at Stage Depot* - Zachery Scott

1952 *Half Breed* - Jack Butel and Robert Young

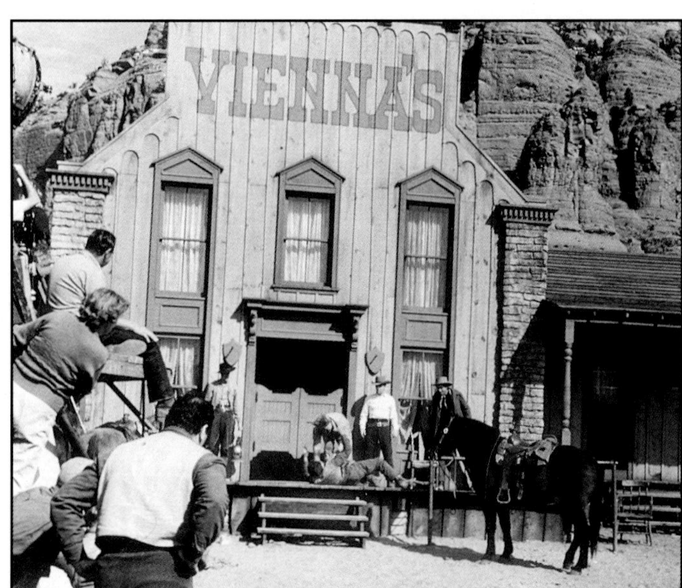

1953 *Johnny Guitar* - Vienna's Bar

1953 *Johnny Guitar* - Ernest Borgnine and Scott Brady playing the bad guys opposite Sterling Hayden and Joan Crawford.

Bob Bradshaw Autobiography

One of Babcock's mares enjoys a drink of Bobby Jr.'s bathwater behind our camera store.

Our neighbor, Shirley, who recently retired as manager of Bank One.

I doubled as one of the badmen in *The Last Wagon*.

I played a Cavalry Soldier on *Yellowstone Kelly* starring Clint Walker.

Captain Rynning from the TV show *Twenty Six Men*

We did a lot of filming for television around Sedona, but no one had a TV set in town. We had to go to Cottonwood to view what we had filmed.

The stagecoach passes the base of Bell Rock on the TV series *Twenty Six Men*.

The show was about the Arizona Rangers.

This 4-horse team belonged to me at the time.

The Forest Service tore down Call Of The Canyon Resort and put up a parking lot.

Sedona Lodge

These are part of a brochure I photographed in 1950 for Royal Palms Inn.

"Fun in the Sun" in the late 40s, early 50s, became the tourism slogan for Arizona.
These commercial photographs I took during that era were part of a national advertising campaign.

Bob Bradshaw Autobiography

Paradise Inn – Camelback Road, Scottsdale

Casablanca Hotel – Phoenix, AZ

Los Caballeros Ranch – Wickenburg, AZ

Flying "E" Ranch – Wickenburg, AZ

KL/Bar Ranch – Wickenburg, AZ

Castle Hot Springs - Wickenburg, AZ

Hacienda Del Sol Ranch Hotel – Tucson, AZ

This was taken in the 50's. This olympic size pool at Call Of The Canyon was later covered over by the Forest Service.

Bob Bradshaw Autobiography

Beaver Creek Dude Ranch

Adventures on the Ranch

When I bought the ranch in 1960, everyone said I was crazy to pay $200 an acre. That always brings a smile to my face when I think about it. Now it's worth $50,000 an acre. Bradshaw Ranch is located 12 miles from Sedona and is at the junction of Hartwell Canyon and Loy Canyon.

It was an old homestead, which had been abandoned in 1942. Nothing was left except the old adobe house and a bunch of rickety board shacks. While clearing out the shacks, which were full of rattlesnakes, I found a rattler that was 6 feet long. That was the biggest rattler I'd ever seen before or since.

Jack Cox and his wife, Grace, homesteaded this land in the 30's. Jack Cox made his living growing and selling produce from his land while raising their two boys, Bob and Ed. To give you an idea of what the life was like for them, just to keep the trees alive, they had to travel over a mile with horse and wagon to Taylor Tank to fill up three fifty gallon barrels with water, travel back to the ranch and water the one thousand trees by hand. Three barrels was enough water for only three trees. Imagine how long that took to complete the task.

In 1942, Jack's wife got tired of the difficult lifestyle and the family moved out. Among the things they abandoned 18 years prior to my taking it over was this large orchard near the adobe house. Two or three of the fruit trees managed to live without water all those years and are still living today along with a new orchard I planted.

There were no fences and the make-shift corrals were in ruins. I certainly had my work cut out for me. I employed a well driller and got a good well at 320 feet. I bought a second hand windmill in Winslow and installed it over the well. Then I hired three Indians from Montana to help me build a 3-mile fence around the ranch. We cut 1000 cedar posts in the forest 30 miles north of Flagstaff and hauled them to Sedona in an old 1935 ton and a half Ford truck. Digging 1000 postholes in every type of terrain imaginable was no picnic. At the tops of the hills, the soil was rocky and almost impossible to dig into. Using a digging bar was the only way to do it. A lot of the holes in the west fence line had to be blasted out of solid rock. Down in the flats, the going was easy because the soil was nice and sandy.

I remember the weather that season. It was January and most of the time it was too hot to wear a shirt. Once the fences were complete, the Indians left and I started building the arena and corrals. I was very fortunate at the time because everything from the old smelter at Clarkdale, which had been shut down in 1956, was for sale. They had piles of brand new railroad ties with all new saturated tar in them. 15-ft switch ties sold for $1.50 and regular 8-ft ties for $1. The switch ties were my gateposts and the regulars were posts for the arena and corrals.

After all this was done, I decided to buy a good quarter horse stallion and some mares from Babbitt's Spider Web Ranch in Flagstaff. The mares were very wild. The Babbitt cowboys ran the two mares I picked out up the chute to my truck. The mares could hardly stand up because of the metal floor in my new truck so I threw some dirt into the truck with a shovel. The mares exploded as if they had been blown up with dynamite. I finally got them to the ranch and turned them out. It was common knowledge in northern Arizona that all of the Spider Web mares were descendents of Clabber Boy, the Babbitt Ranch stallion. Clabber boy was a chronic bucker and had passed this trait on to all of his colts. Anyone who raised colts from Clabber boy mares had bucking colts to contend with. Just to halter break these two mares was a lot of work. My neighbor Joe Robinson came down to help me fore foot each mare. This is when you catch their front feet in your loop forcing the horse to go down and you jump on the head and body. While they are down you put on a halter with a lead rope on them. You then take a big soft rope and tie it

The windmill silhouette
against the blazing sunset
at Bradshaw Ranch

My two nieces, Dawn and Cindy, overlooking the entire ranch area.

80 year old Adobe House at Bradshaw Ranch

(as is shown in the photograph on page 83) to pull up a back leg. With one back leg off the ground, the horse is helpless. You sack out the horse using canvas or burlap (see page 82). This gets a wild horse used to being touched by humans.

Now comes the time to turn the horse out into the arena. First you put a long 30-ft. rope on the halter. Then, you tie the end to a heavy switch tie or a log (see page 82). Just when the horse thinks it is free and running away, she comes to the end of the rope and falls to the ground. The railroad tie or log gives just enough so it doesn't hurt the horse. A few tries like this and the horse will learn not to run off. With a gentle horse, it's a different story. You can teach a 10-day-old colt to lead in a few minutes by using a small halter with a lead rope. You put the loop of a lariat on the colt's rear end, pull on it when the colt gives to the lariat, and you can lead at the same time. When the horse has this mastered pretty well, you can take the lariat off of his butt. Another way is to lead the mother and colt together. In one of the photos, you can see that the colt is actually following his mother but is learning to lead at the same time (see page 82).

After a while, the wild mares were all trimmed and fat. I raised a total of 20 colts from these mares. I named the Bay mare's first colt, Hosteen (Navajo word for mister), and I would still be riding him today if he didn't die from eating the wrong feed where he was boarded in 1998.

Another horse I inherited from a neighbor is a story in itself. Wayne Williams was the watchman at Windmill Ranch, who at the time was dying from chronic asthma. He had a horse trailer that I was trying to buy from him and a horse he bought in Texas named Buck. He wouldn't sell the trailer unless I took the horse. He wanted Buck to have a good home, so he sold me the horse trailer for $400 and I inherited Buck. At that time, I didn't know what a great horse he would turn out to be. He was four when I got him and 30 when he died. Buck was one of the most versatile horses in the world; he was a good ranch horse, a gentle kid's horse, a great horse for trail riding dudes and a perfect horse to use in the movies. You will see him in action throughout this story of the ranch. All of the directors and producers liked Buck because of his conformation, color and personality.

Buck was the first Marlboro horse in the first commercial with Roy Sickner. Roy was the first Marlboro man on television when cigarettes were still allowed on the picture tube. Since then, Buck worked on the following commercials, feature pictures and TV shows. Vicks Cough Drops was next. The director wanted to use me as the cowboy, but instead the producer brought someone from New York. The idea of the commercial was pretty funny. The cowboy is watching the herd of 100 cows and has a coughing fit. The cows all stampede, the actor pulls out the cough drops and everything is supposed to be OK. All the actor had to do was fall in behind the cattle. We stampeded the cattle and this guy went the opposite direction. Then they yelled for me to put on his clothes and double for him on the second take. His resume and composite listed 'excellent horseman and stunt rider' under his skills. He made about $40,000 in residuals and I made $25 to ride Buck that day. It happens that way sometimes.

Then we did a Mazola Corn Oil commercial, Wrigley's Big Red gum, Old Chap Jeans with a Spanish Production Company, Cudahy Bar S, Falstaff Beer with Sam Elliott, Lucky Lagers Beer, Arm and Hammer Baking Soda, Big Sur Cigars, Golden Graham Cereals, Britannia Jeans, Acme Boots, Xerox, a popular Japanese men's face lotion with me and Bronson, and finally, a Marlboro commercial for Hong Kong.

Joe dodging switchties

Bertha is the mean, wild horse that bit a piece out of Bobby's arm.

I'm ground-driving
and Bobby Jr.
is leading.

Horse hobbled to show procedure

Me on Buck driving Hosteen

Top: Two received Mares

Bottom: Hank at Red Corral

Bob Bradshaw Autobiography

Top: Me riding Hank

Bottom: Bertha and baby Hosteen when the colt was sorrel

Buck was the model in these magazine ads and stories as well: Mercury automobiles, Playboy, July '71, Mademoiselle, May '82, Vogue Magazine with at the time, world famous model, Verushka.

Buck also played in these television movies: *Death Valley Days*, *Wilderness Road*, *Westward Wagons*, *Body and Soul* with Linda Carter, and finally, *Images of Indians*. Buck worked more than most stars and played in these feature films, too. In December of '66, *Fire Creek* (I doubled Jim Best on Buck), then *Thunder Warrior*, and in December of '79, *Revenge of a Killer*.

The 1960's and 1970's brought many productions to the ranch area and Sedona. I continued to do my job as location man, contact man and coordinator. Many locations were used on and around Bradshaw Ranch. In 1961, I helped scout out the locations for a movie called *The Legend of Lobo*. A lot of the scenes were filmed around Bradshaw Ranch. One scene was shot at the Indian Ruins in Red Canyon. The company had two wolves for most of the close-ups and 45 wolves were kept at the ranch, which is now the beautiful Sedona Pines Resort.

I made a deal in 1967 with Emery Vickers to buy his 30-head cow permit in Boynton Canyon for 7 months in the winter. In the summer, I took the cattle to Hart Prairie 10 miles out of Flagstaff. The registered bull I bought from MGM was responsible for the excellent herd of Hereford cattle I have had all these years (see page 92).

About this time in my marriage, Bea decided she wanted a divorce. Her chain smoking was damaging her health and I pressured her to quit smoking so much, she finally quit me instead. We had been married for twenty-five years.

Shortly after that divorce, I met Marie Jackson. She was a beautiful, tall blonde in her early twenties. Marie was very good at helping around the ranch. She helped build fences and was good with the horses. She was an extra in *Stay Away Joe* and a few other films we worked on together.

Stay Away Joe, starring Elvis Presley, was quite an adventure. The Director, Peter Tewksbury, said he was looking for a river crossing with a vista. I told him that there was no such thing in Sedona. But I had an idea and asked him to come with me to my ranch and I'd show him how he could have what he was looking for. I brought him to the edge of a dry wash on the central part of the ranch that had a fantastic view behind it. I said, "If you fill this wash with water, you can create what you're after right here." He studied it for a few minutes, nodded his head and said, "Yeah, you're right, Bob, this is the place." My horse arena was within a hundred yards of the principle set and this was another benefit for the production.

With Elvis in town, the red rocks were buzzing with electricity. I found a house for him to stay in below King's Ransom on Oak Creek. I found another place for his Memphis Mafia entourage near by. Colonel Parker stayed out on Jordan Road and Navahopi, and Elvis's maid and cook had their own house, too. Security was a big thing and most of us weren't used to that kind of protection. There were two deputies on duty all the time. The movie took two and a half months to be completed. Elvis was a nice guy, very down to earth and seemed to enjoy the process of filmmaking in Sedona. We bought the huge poster of *Stay Away Joe* with all the cast and crew autographs covering the paper and had it at the ranch for all the tourists to enjoy. Unfortunately in 2001, someone stole it off the wall. We're offering a huge reward for its return since it is invaluable to our family and the Bradshaw Ranch heritage. Any information about it should be directed to my son, John….no questions asked.

1966 *Cimmaron Strip* - I played Captain of the Guard and my orders were
to throw Richard Boone in jail. Marie played an extra on the set.

I married Marie shortly after the completion of filming *Stay Away Joe*. We had two little boys, John and Scott, within a couple of years. I still made very little money in those years even though it was a pretty interesting life involved with the entertainment industry. I couldn't even afford to pay the doctor when the boys were born, so I traded a colt for each son's birth. A big part of this book will be about the boys and how they grew up learning about horses and cattle and how to be ranch hands. Their adventures would make a great kid's book or television series, that's for sure.

The weather in the winter of '67 was long and bitter for Sedona. We had 30 inches of snow at the ranch and on the 12-mile dirt road into town. It was one of the worst winters in Sedona on record and one we would never forget.

In 1968, the only record I have of any production was a Vogue Magazine job. The most famous model at that time was Countess Verushka. She was in Sedona to do a feature story for Vogue. I helped her photographer, Franco Rubartelli, find all the locations photographed in the June '68 issue.

We filmed a pilot for TV in 1969 called *Wilderness Road*. I was the location manager for NBC and was given credit on the titles, which is always exciting to see on the big screen. I furnished all the horses and wrangled them to different areas. The film was about a rancher-photographer, who had two kids who lived with him on the ranch. I thought it was a great idea for a series because people could learn about ranch life and the different scenic areas of the country where the rancher-photographer went to his photography assignments. He also took the kids with him on many of his assignments. I often thought how easy this part would be for me to play since I am a rancher-photographer all the time and, of course, I had two kids. I would just have to play myself and the dialogue would come easy.

That year, I also worked on a TV show called *Then Came Bronson*, starring Michael Parks. My job was to help the producer find all of the locations for two episodes.

Early in 1970, ABC Television began production for *This Land Is Mine*. The crew had been interviewing people across America and filming them for their TV special. The theme of the show was to ask people why they lived where they live. One of the production teams called me and asked me to suggest an idea for a segment. When they asked who would be good to interview in Sedona, I said, "Why don't you use the cowboy artists? They can live anywhere to do their paintings. You can ask them why they live in Sedona." Lester Cooper, the producer, thought it was a good idea. I called three artists who belonged to the Cowboy Artists of America; Jim Reynolds, Charlie Dye and Joe Beeler. We all met at the Reynolds place in the Village of Oak Creek. The crew spent a couple of hours interviewing the artists and then asked me to go to the ranch with them for an interview of me on camera. I was surprised they wanted to interview me. I called Ira Smith to help me gather some calves out at the ranch for the shoot and for a while, we drove them around for the cameras. Then they put a microphone in my shirt and asked me to follow the camera car on my horse while they asked me questions.

The crew left Sedona and went back to edit and do post-production before airing the segment. In the meantime, Jim, Charlie and Joe were telling everyone to watch for them on the show. The day before it was scheduled to air, I received a letter from Cooper telling me to watch ABC at a certain time. I was surprised when there was no sign of any artists on the program, only Ira and I at the ranch avoided the cutting room floor. ABC sent me a tape of the show. After they left Sedona, they went to Big Sur and Carmel to interview Kim Novak and film her riding a horse for the next segment.

Me and Elvis during *Stay Away Joe*

Elvis Presley Rodeo – Arena at Bradshaw Ranch

Verushka models for Vogue at Bradshaw Ranch

While everybody is freezing in their winter clothes, Verushka is in a flimsy spring dress modeling next season's fashions.

Horses and Cattle

My 20 heifers and 10 cows on Hart Prairie. I did all of the cow punching myself until the boys were old enough to help.

In April 1970, I scoured locations for two Kal-Kan commercials. One location was to resemble Africa because the commercial was about a cheetah. I remember we had to move all of the cattle out of the surrounding area because the cheetah would chase them. To get the cat to run across the screen, a live chicken was put on a stick and the cheetah would run to it (70 miles an hour makes the cheetah the fastest land animal). At the end of the run, the cat would be roped with a lariat. When they had enough takes by the end of the day, the chicken was given to the Cheetah as a reward. The commercial shows the Cheetah eating out of a Kal Kan bowl. The other Kal Kan commercial was with a mountain lion and the same routine was used with a chicken on a stick up on Schnebly Hill.

Later that year, we also filmed a Mac Leans Toothpaste commercial at Slide Rock in Oak Creek Canyon. Then in June of 1970, I went to Monument Valley to wrangle a horse for Charles Bronson. The commercial was for some famous Japanese men's face lotion products. During a break, Bronson was trying to tip over the top of a huge mushroom shaped rock when Sam Day from the Navajo tribal council showed up. Sam hollered at him. "I wouldn't do that if I were you." If Bronson had yelled back we would have been thrown out. Instead, Bronson looked at the rock and looked back at Sam Day. "Somebody else might like to see that rock the way it is", Sam emphasized. Bronson looked back at the rock and then at Sam Day and said, "I guess you're right." Bronson left the rock alone and went over to sit with his wife, Jill Ireland, and his kids.

Another job I worked on in 1970 was a still ad for Yardley Cosmetics. They called me from New York and asked me to round up a few 35-year-old cowboys for them to look at. When the production crew arrived in Sedona, I approached the casting director. "What's wrong with me?" I asked. "Not a damn thing!" they said, and I got the job. I was 52 years old at the time and I was to play the Lone Ranger on a white horse they were bringing up from Phoenix. Their model was supposed to sit on the saddle in front of me. The first time I tried to get on the white horse, he tried to buck me off. So with the tall blonde and me in position, I had to manage that horse for the rest of the day to stay still enough for a focused still shot.

I scouted locations with Ira Lassman, Tom Duffy and the Director/Cameraman, Lucien Ballard, Cinematographer of John Wayne's *Rooster Cogburn* for the Acme Boot commercial. They choose Bradshaw Ranch and Red Rock Crossing for locations. They spent a week in Los Angeles trying to find someone that could look the part of a cowboy. The person they chose didn't look like a cowboy at all. He rode a horse with his feet sticking out in front of him like he was water skiing or riding a motorcycle. He kept bragging how good a rodeo hand he was, but he didn't know that the still men were coming to do the print ads and they wanted him to catch a calf and tie it up. So we gave him a rope, put a horse out in the arena with a calf and told him to go catch the calf. Then the "big rodeo man" said, "I can't do that". We had to tie up the calf for him so he could pretend to be a cowboy for the stills. One of the best shots in the commercial was the horse splashing through the water at Red Rock Crossing.

In 1971, Universal was filming *The Bravos*, a pilot for TV starring George Peppard. The executive producer called and asked me to check out the set at Leupp, Arizona (45 miles north of Flagstaff). It was the adobe fort we used in Cimmaron Strip. I called him back and said that it was in excellent condition. He told me to meet the unit manager at the Flagstaff airport the next day. So, the next day I went to Flagstaff a little early and sat in a restaurant to kill time. In walked a guy from the Chamber of Commerce who thought *he* was the location man. We got to talking and he said he was waiting for some people from Universal to come into the airport. To say the least, I was confused. So I called the executive producer to ask him if he wanted me or

The advertising agency called me from New York City and asked me to gather a number of models around 35 years of age that could ride a horse so their casting director could take a look at them when they got here. I decided to take a chance and not call anybody for the audition. Instead, when they got into town, and they asked me where the models were, I said, "Well, what about hiring me to play the Lone Ranger?" I was 52 at the time. The director paused, looked me up and down and replied, "Ok, Bob, you'll do just fine."

By then, I was married to Marie who wasn't too thrilled to see another blonde as tall as she was sitting on the saddle with me for the entire day. Marie flashed her blue eyes at me and said, "Just remember, Bob, I'm keepin' my eye on you!" I could feel the New York model move an inch away from me in the saddle.

The agency must have been happy with the results, because the director sent me a 16x20 reprint of the ad that had been placed in millions of magazines throughout the country.

In 1967, we went
into the business
of raising cows.
We bought this bull
from MGM after
Stay Away Joe
starring
Elvis Presley.

My granddaughter, Jami, Hosteen and me

Jami wasn't even
afraid of
the bull.

Shiny Hosteen

While I was building the barn, Hank was doing his thing.

the man from the Chamber of Commerce to go to the fort. He was pretty upset that the unit manager went over his head. He told me to go to the airport and he would take care of the situation. When I got to the airport, Joe, the unit manager, was mad that I went over his head. I paid no attention to him and went about my job. We scouted the fort at Leupp and Schnebly Hill in Sedona. The director was very happy with my knowledge of the area and my experience in motion pictures. When he came back to Sedona, he gave me a part in the picture.

When they came back to film, the unit manager tried to get even with me by using the Chamber of Commerce guy as much as possible. His office was in Flagstaff and while he was up there, a big wet snow came along (about 8 inches). I called him and said I had a man standing by for hire with a grader to push the snow aside. He gave me a real smart answer, "We're having the county clear that snow for nothing." I guess it was something the Chamber of Commerce guy had arranged. Anyway, the snow never got cleared that day and that night the temperature went to zero and turned that wet snow to solid ice. Now, with the roads inaccessible, everything would have to be transported up the hill with Jeeps and the horses would have to be ridden up on the ice. The next morning, the temperature was still zero and the wind was blowing hard. Believe me, we earned our money sitting on a horse all day in that weather for the rest of the shoot. I had chosen the men who played the cavalry soldiers; I had the part of the sergeant. It is a good thing I chose all good cowboys because we had to lope up through the ice with sabers and guns and flags. The horses could just barely stand up. I had to pass a Sharps rifle to another officer on camera. Then we rode to the base of Merry-Go-Round Rock where we staged shooting Indians off the top. In the story, the Indians captured George Peppard's son and we were trying to get him back.

While all this was going on, the unit manager was up in his office and had hired a girl to interview prospective cavalrymen for the sequences at the fort. After her initial selection, she sent their pictures down to the assistant director for review. I will never forget the look on his face when he came out of the office. He had a big smile on his face and said, "I just picked out all the cavalry soldiers." I thought to myself, "You moron. You have to audition a guy on a horse if he is supposed to *ride* a horse." To take his word that he's a good rider is subjective at best. I wasn't part of the first fort segment, but I heard through the grapevine that the filming at the fort was a complete disaster because these guys couldn't ride and kept falling off their horses.

Right about the time I was supposed to go to the fort, MGM came in with another project. I was glad to quit Universal so I could work with MGM. MGM was making the feature film, *The Wild Rovers*. I spent a week with the producer, cameraman and unit manager looking for locations. The Director, Blake Edwards, showed up the day before we were supposed to shoot to choose one of the key locations for the scene where Bill Holden and Ryan O'Neal catch a mare out of a wild herd of horses and then break her to ride. We all got in Blake's helicopter and went to all the places we had picked out. The place they liked for the herd was my ranch. So we landed the chopper for Blake to check it out. He looked at it awhile and said, "This is where we start tomorrow."

We went back to the hotel to get ready for the first day's shooting schedule. That night, Blake called us together and said, "I changed my mind. We're going to do the horse breaking in the snow on the Frisco Peaks." It was a good decision because some of the most dramatic shots were made in the snow. The tough part was rearranging all the people and equipment to the Flagstaff area forty miles away.

1970 *Wilderness Road* – NBC

1970 *Wild Rovers* – NBC

Horses on a rare snow
day at the ranch

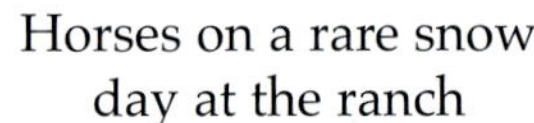

The big snow of 1967, on the ranch road. Walter Hurley went ahead of Ernie with a bullgozer through the 30 inches of snow. There were 40 inches in Cottonwood that caved in all the fragile roofs that were not used to heavy snow. Jerome had 50 inches. Gold King Mine had 60 inches.

Ernie McMinnamon, pictured below, was on the grader.

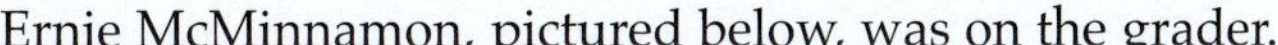

Bobby shoveling snow off the adobe roof – His own place on the Hidden Valley Road was snowbound for many days.

Adobe house in the snow

The next day, I got in the helicopter with Blake Edwards, the cameraman, and the associate producer. The first location I suggested on Hart Prairie ten miles outside of Flagstaff was O.K. with the director. We went back to Sedona to prepare for the next day. It was a good thing I knew every foot of the Hart Prairie area so I could do a good job of scouting from the air.

We headed up there and worked for a week in 18 inches of snow. The results on film were spectacular. For the bronco ride, they had 15 bay horses and they put each horse through three times so they had a total of 45 rides on film. They over cranked and made these shots in slow motion. There were four cameras on every ride. In my opinion, this was the best bronc-ride ever captured on film. Floyd Baze was the cowboy stunt man that rode 45 consecutive times. Back in Sedona, we worked at Red Rock Crossing, Bradshaw Ranch and several other good locations. Then we went to Monument Valley to finish the picture.

I had a tough assignment in 1971. I was working with Pompeo Posar on a playboy magazine feature with Clair Rambeau. I had to wrangle Claire's horse for a week and watch all the skinny-dipping and naked posing up on Schnebly Hill. The cars were lined up on the road above Merry-Go-Round Rock. A small crowd of men, manned with binoculars, was having the time of their lives. The story came out in the Playboy, October 1971 issue.

In 1972, some people from New York made a deal with us to build an 1870 western town on the south forty of our ranch for production companies to use. They financed the construction on our land and we split the profits fifty/fifty. I was busy that year training colts for the various production possibilities that venture instigated.

Nosey, the Sweetest Skunk in the West was a television movie of the week we made that year. Richard Lyford was the Director for Disney Studios. It took us a year to produce this one-hour show. My first job was to show Lyford the best locations to film. My second job was to find local people to act in the film. Janie Biddle got the lead because of her natural interest in animals. Verdon Hollis from Cottonwood was cast as the father. A Sedona artist, Walter Carlson, was cast as the banker, and Lois Binford played Carlson's wife. We spent a few weeks filming with Verdon Hollis, but for some reason, a disagreement between Hollis and the director came up and he quit. He had to be replaced by the Hollywood actor, Jim Chandler, and we had to do the same shots over again with Chandler. The principal set was out at Bell Rock and was the trailer home of Janie and her father. Her father is an artist and they lived out in the country where he painted scenic landscapes.

There was a scene in which I was doing the stunt work. I can still remember some of these professional stunt men telling the director how tough the stunt was going to be. I just got into the car and did what the director asked me to do. The scene took place when the banker went out to see some of the artists' paintings. He pulls up to the trailer in his Lincoln Continental and leaves the motor running. While he is gone, his wife is sitting in the passenger side with two poodle dogs in her lap. The poodles see Janie's pet skunk and go crazy trying to get out of the car. They accidentally flip the gearshift into reverse and the car crashes over a cliff and into the river. It was my job to double the banker's wife. I got dressed in the wife's clothes in my size and got in on the passenger side of the car. I put my left hand on the wheel, my left foot on the brakes and careened off this steep hill heading for the creek at top speed without looking back so my face wasn't seen on camera. I managed to get out of the sinking car, save the two poodles, and swim to safety with the dogs. In this part of the story, the dogs get lost and everyone is searching for them. By the time this picture was finished, I was pretty tired of wrangling poodle dogs and skunks.

1973 was another good production year; we did four commercials and one magazine ad. The first one was for Cudahy Bar S Ham. We shot a lot of outdoor western scenes. I guess it was supposed to prove that cowboys eat ham. They put all local people in it and actor-singer Rex Allen narrated it. It was filmed up in the high country near Williams, Arizona. I furnished the horses, wagons and extras. During this shoot, I remember another guy and I were riding to the barn. They came directly over our head with a helicopter to get their aerial shots. I was riding Buck; the chopper didn't bother him a bit. The other guy's horse was good, too. Having horses that can handle the noise and sight of a helicopter is pretty rare.

In April of '73, we did four Falstaff Beer commercials. The theme was a take-off on *The Rounders* movie with sidekicks Glenn Ford and Henry Fonda. Falstaff Beer teamed up Sam Elliott and Mike Whitney to play buddies on all of their commercials. We worked at Red Rock Crossing, Dry Creek, the Hi Low Ranch, and an old barn on the Loop Road. I scouted locations and furnished the horses and mules.

Later that year in July, a production company came in to do a Xerox commercial. The idea of the commercial was to show that Xerox salesmen go everywhere. They started filming at our movie town. This was supposed to be the place that the Xerox salesman meets the Indian boy who is supposed to guide him into the Havasupai Village in the Grand Canyon. The Indian showed up with two mules for them to ride. I had two mules at the ranch, but the director insisted on using Havasupai mules, so I had to drive all the way to the Grand Canyon to get them. I called the Indian agent before I left to ask if these mules were trailer broke. He said that they were, so I headed to Peach Springs and north to the Havasupai Reservation. They had the mules waiting for me at the top of the rim, but neither mule had ever seen a horse trailer before. It took about 8 people to shove them in the trailer. We had mule trek shots in various places, which meant we had to transport them by trailer, but I wasn't too keen about loading these untrained critters. By the time I got through working with them throughout the production, you could point them at a trailer ten feet away and they would run into it. We filmed at the Chinle Hills near Cameron, and the weird Red Rock monuments near Tuba City. After that, I took the mules back to the Indians at the canyon. When they got the mules back, they were surely trailer broken.

The fourth commercial of 1973 was not successful. It was an International Truck commercial filmed on the road near Bradshaw Ranch. The commercial was a contest, between the International truck driver and another truck company, to make a long jump between two ramps. It was eleven feet to the top of the ramps and 20 some feet between them. Stuntman Hal Needham was ready to do the stunt with the International Truck when they got word from the factory that there were some inferior parts in the prototype. A prototype is often used in car commercials and is put together before regular manufacturing has started on the model. Prototypes are put together poorly. Hal Needham couldn't wait another day until the parts were replaced, so he went back to Hollywood and sent another stuntman out to do the job. The next day, the truck was ready. The light was right, the crew was all set and the new driver was behind the wheel. The speed was estimated for the jump and the director called for "action." The new driver got heavy footed and took the ramp too fast. The truck cleared the second ramp completely and plowed into the hard road nose first, totally wiping out the $45,000 prototype and wrecking the stuntman's back. When anything like this happens you couldn't do it over again and show it. It was against FFA Rules. So, the whole thing was a bust for them.

The magazine ad I did in 1973 was an ad for Mercury cars. My cattle were running in Boynton Canyon at the time, so that's where we shot the ad. We had my cattle all around the

THE QUARTER HORSE JOURNAL
MARCH, 1968 • 50¢

Mercury car, which demonstrated the easy nature of my stock. Most cows would have been very unmanageable for that kind of shoot.

In 1974, we made a movie called *Survival*. It was the story of a family that crash lands in a Bonanza Airplane. In the script, everyone is injured except the young boy. They used the south side of the runway at the airport to fake the crash site. From there you can see Jerome in the distance. The story is about the boy and his adventures trying to get to Jerome for help. A mountain lion is following him most of the way. I got some of my cowboy friends to play possemen and we set out on horseback to find the lion. The boy finally reaches Jerome and ends up at the Little Daisy, which is a derelict hotel. The lion is still stalking the boy through the rooms. At the point where he leaps to attack the boy, a deputy, who has been trying to find the sheriff, shoots the lion. With the lion taken care of, they go into the basement of the hotel and find the sheriff in a den of rattlesnakes. It is an exciting film produced by Mark IV Pictures, directed by Donald Thompson, starring Robby Sella, Terry Griffin and Peach Braaten.

We also did a Coca-Cola commercial in '74. This one called for a situation that I had to scout out a barn for square dancers to shoot the commercial. While all of this filming activity was going on, my boys were getting bigger and learning a lot about cattle, horses and ranching. We seldom left our ranch and movie life, but in May of 1975, I took the boys to the zoo in Phoenix, which was quite a change for them from the ranch. This was their first time in a city. They got to experience a lot of unusual animals they didn't see in Arizona.

I was hired as talent in May of 1975, and was sent to Florida to play a Tobacco Farmer in an ad for the American Tobacco Institute. A lot of guys in Hollywood auditioned for the role, but the director happened to see a photograph of me and insisted that the casting director track me down for the part. They flew me to Jacksonville, Florida to shoot part of it and then to the best tobacco fields on the Georgia border. Even though I didn't smoke in real life, this ended up on my resume.

We made an Arm and Hammer Baking Soda commercial at Bradshaw Ranch that July. The shoot required us to create an 1850 cow camp with a chuck wagon, bedrolls, saddles, cowboys and horses. I helped the director and prop man come up with all of this stuff. I also helped cast the cowboys. They made me the foreman of the camp and I rode up to the chuck wagon on my horse, Hosteen (the horse I raised from a colt). The line was "Arm and Hammer has been settling stomachs for 125 years." Then I go over to the cook and get the baking soda and drink it down. By the end of all of the takes, I was the one *with* a stomachache!

In August of 1975, we had a job for Golden Graham Cereal. They needed horses as close to cereal colors as possible. The location was Schnebly Hill and the set up was a family camping on Merry-Go-Round Rock.

1976 was another busy year. We did four commercials and one movie. Two of the commercials were for Honda. We shot one for Sunbeam Bread and one for Mazola Corn Oil. The Sunbeam Bread people called me from Phoenix to ask if they could use the ranch horses and cowboys. They said they were casting a little boy in Phoenix who was to play the leading role. The plot of the commercial was to show the little boy eating bread in a fancy kitchen back east and then show him on a fence at the ranch where he wishes he *could* be. I told them I would find a fancy kitchen in Sedona for their opening location. When they met me at my trailer in Sunset Park, I was walking out of the house with John. The minute they saw John they all broke into smiles. They had found their little star. John worked in the fancy kitchen, then at the ranch

Firecreek starring Henry Fonda. Cameras are rolling as Henry Fonda leads the way.

I doubled for Jim Best in *Firecreek*. Jim Best, known for his role as the Deputy on *The Dukes of Hazard*.

sitting on the fence eating bread. Then, a cowboy, Don Bryson, rides up and swings John into the saddle in front of him and ropes a calf out of the arena. John was so at home in a ranch setting, I doubt that they would have ever found a better kid for the part.

The fourth commercial we worked on in 1976 was for Mazola Corn Oil which was the story of a family riding horseback and then having a picnic. It was shot at Bradshaw Ranch and I supplied the horses and some of the picnickers.

The TV movie we did in '76 was *Westward Wagons*. We worked at Bradshaw Ranch, Hart Prairie, Flagstaff, and the Buffalo Range east of Flagstaff. I furnished the three wagons and the canvas covers. My friend, J.T. Pritchard, furnished the horse teams. They cast me in the part of the wagon master and I used my good horse, Hosteen, to lead the wagons.

Later in 1976, we did the Elvis Presley film on the ranch called *Stay Away Joe*. We shot a major portion of that picture for two and a half months on Bradshaw Ranch.

1977 was another year for productions. We did a movie for TV, two commercials, and a magazine ad. The movie was *Relentless* starring Will Sampson, Larry Wilcox, Monte Markham, David Pendelton, Marianna Hill, John Hillerman, John Lawler and Anthony Ponzine. The story centers around a bank robbery, which was filmed at Valley National Bank in Camp Verde where a bank guard is shot. Will Sampson and Larry Wilcox are highway patrolman and are sent to the bank to investigate the incident. The dead bank guard is Will Sampson's uncle and the rest of the story is his pursuit of the killers. They locate the place where the van left the road and found the tracks of an airplane taking off. The airplane crashed at Taylor tank near Bradshaw Ranch. John Hillerman (who later played Higgins in Magnum, P.I.) is the leader of the outlaws. He "booby traps" the plane with wires and dynamite. When the FBI man investigates, he is blown up with the plane. CBS flew a twin-engine plane to Sedona just to blow it up for the film. The rest of the film shows Will Sampson using his Indian skills to track down the killers (Will Sampson is famous for playing the big Indian part in *One Flew Over the Cuckoos Nest*).

The two commercials we worked on in 1977 were for Ford Bronco trucks and Schlitz Beer. The Bronco commercial was filmed at Don Hoel's Cabins and Courthouse Rock. It was about a bunch of mountain climbers gassing up the truck at Don Hoel's gas pumps in Oak Creek Canyon. I played the gas station attendant.

The Schlitz Beer commercial was a disaster for a couple of reasons. It seemed like the crew was "on something" because they just couldn't seem to get it together. And if that wasn't enough, they ran into bad weather during the shoot. The commercial involved four cowboys, two packhorses and 25 wild horses. My indication that the crew was acting goofy was when I called in all of my good cowboys to try out for the principal part. The director asked me to find a small Mexican man that could ride and rope. Our state stock inspector at that time matched the description exactly and he had the skills to do the job. After the interview with the Mexican man, one of the crewmen asked the director why he didn't hire the guy. I heard the director say, "He's too diminutive." They found a Mexican man in Los Angeles who looked just like the stock inspector of about the same height, but he couldn't ride or rope. The scenes they shot with him didn't work because he couldn't handle the requirements and the footage ended up on the cutting room floor.

The director also cast most of the cowboys out of Los Angeles. One of them sued the company for hurting his back when he fell out of a truck. The whole job was a complete fiasco. They were filming the cowboys and packhorses coming through a pass near the Woo Ranch.

Henry Fonda and me during the filming of *Fire Creek*

The idea of the commercial was for the cowboys to see a bunch of wild horses; one has a wire on its leg and is dragging some brush along with him. The cowboys decide to catch the horse and cut the wire off of his leg. The shot of the men coming through the pass and seeing the horses took all morning to film. The lunch wagon was a mile away. I couldn't figure out why it was set up that far away. While we were watching the herd, the assistant director came over to me and asked if I could take half of the men and ride our horses to the lunch wagon. I thought this was pretty stupid because there was a vehicle right there that could have taken us to the lunch wagon. The assistant director said to come back after we had eaten and relieve the other wranglers so they could eat. I didn't question anything because I thought they knew what they were doing. We rode over to the lunch wagon, had our lunch and went back to the location to relieve the other wranglers. When the assistant director saw us, he got all fired up and asked, "What did you ride your horses back for?" I told him that was what we were told to do. It turned out that they wanted all the horses to stay at the lunch wagon for a shot near there after lunch. That miscommunication wasn't our fault, yet we lost a lot of time because the assistant director left a small but critical detail out. What that cost the production company was the afternoon shoot in the schedule. The next day, it rained so hard that they all decided to go back to New York and reschedule the filming at a later date.

When I received the call from New York with the new shooting date. I ordered more hay for the horses and trucked 25 of them into the ranch. We got the 25 horses and the trailer with the wild bronco they wanted to use for close-ups to the location and the filming began. We stampeded the horses for the actors to fall behind and rope them by the camera. The first close-up was the Hollywood Mexican roping a horse. Instead, he got the rope around his own neck. On the second stampede, he lost his hat. They finally gave up on him and let a good cowboy do the roping. In the afternoon, they shot a campfire scene with the actors, but it started to cloud up and it didn't match the sunlight in the rest of the scenes. Then they decided to make it a rain sequence and they sent me to Flagstaff to buy a bunch of yellow rain slickers for the actors. At 11 pm that night, it was pouring rain. I called the assistant director and asked him what he wanted to do about filming in the morning. I was told to get the 25 good horses to the set by 7 am, rain or shine, at the Woo Ranch. This meant that we had to leave Sedona by 5 am. My local wranglers got their horse trailers stuck in the mud and had to unload the horses several times to get to the ranch. The front gate at Hartwell Canyon was running two-feet deep with water at the crossing. We all saddled up in the pouring rain and loaded the bucking bronco in a horse trailer to haul him to the set. The set was about two miles from the ranch. Within a half of a mile of the ranch, the trailer slid into the ditch and totaled the trailor with the bronco for the day. The rest of us gathered the 25 head and raced through the rain for two miles to the location. We sat there on our horses in the pouring rain and nobody showed up to film. It wasn't like we had cell phones in those days. I rode my horse, Hosteen, three miles to the nearest phone and called the hotel. The crew had no intentions of filming, nor did they have the courtesy to let us know of the change in plans. Their excuse was they didn't have a vehicle that could get out to the location. Any pickup or jeep could have made it. Anyway, because they failed to call me before 5 am, they had to pay for all the wranglers and all the horses for the day. I am glad every job wasn't wrought with problems like this one. But it gives you an idea of what it takes sometimes to get a little 30 or 60 second commercial done. They had to reschedule and come back on a good day.

The magazine ad that we did that year was for a product called Ser-ap-is, a medicine made for combating stress. The ad appeared in a medical magazine. The company wanted a big flock of sheep and a Navajo woman to herd them. The ad showed a farmer being held up on the road by the sheep. He had a load of hay on his truck. Then in the same ad, they show the farmer getting his injection of Ser-ap-is in the doctor's office. I found the location for the shot and they used me as the farmer. I told them that Dr. Stountenburg would be a perfect match for the doctor in their layout, but they said a real doctor couldn't be the doctor in their ad. So, we got a real estate salesman instead to play the doctor.

1978 was a big year for commercials. We worked on four commercials and a magazine ad. In January of 1978, we made a commercial called *Old Chap Jeans* for a company from Spain. We thought they meant chaps, like leather cowboy chaps. When the Spanish guys heard us talking about the chaps we wear, they asked us what chaps were. The name of their jeans "old chap" means "old man" jeans. We had a complete cow camp setup at the ranch with chuck wagon, bedroll, saddles, horses and campfire props. Another part of the commercial was filmed at Red Rock Crossing where a cowboy finds a young boy at the crossing and gives him a ride to the nearest farmhouse. My son, John, was cast again for this part. John is supposed to get the farmer to shoe this guys horse. The old house in the picture was at Pioneer Village outside of Phoenix, so we all traveled to Pioneer for this shot.

In May of 1978, we made two Big Red Gum commercials with horses. We also filmed a Miller Beer commercial that year, called the *Bronc Rider* that ends up at beautiful Taylor Tank for the beer drinking shot.

In December of that year, we had a very tough assignment. It was for Westinghouse and we were to show the power of horses and the difficulty in harnessing the power. We brought in 75 head of horses to the ranch. They were supposed to be wild horses that stampeded past the camera with no wranglers in the shot. In order to accomplish this, I rounded up all the good cowboys I could find to run the horses. Half of the men chased the horses past the camera and the other half stopped them after they passed the camera. The director was a mad man and didn't know when to quit. I guess he thought you could run horses for days like they do in the movies. We put up with three days of this exhausting work on both men and horses, and then told him that it was enough. All the big wheels on the shoot offered us more money if we would keep going, but we told them the horses could not take anymore abuse. We suggested that if they waited one day we would run the horses some more, but they didn't go for that idea. The day before this, we had the 75 head on a ridge all in one bunch. They came in with a helicopter and scattered them for 10 miles in every direction. They had been fed at Bradshaw Ranch the night before and fortunately all drifted back into the ranch that night. We didn't have to gather any of them. We had run them at the ranch, run them at Red Rock Crossing and run them at a canyon in Cottonwood. Then for the final shot, we roped them and hitched them to wagons to demonstrate that the power was controlled, just like they wanted for the point in the commercial.

The magazine ad that year was for Airstream trailers. One shot was at Red Rock Crossing and showed the trailer behind two fishermen. I was one model and Ann Jordan was the other. The other ad was shot of me riding a Palomino horse on Schnebly Hill, giving directions to tourists.

1979 brought us two commercials, one TV movie and a feature film called *Revenge of a Killer*. The first commercial was for Marlboro in Hong Kong. Unlike America, China can show cigarette ads on TV. They set up situations with six of us local cowboys working in Boynton Canyon, Red canyon, Frisco Peaks and Wickenburg. The idea of the commercial was to show 30 head of horses in a corral. In the storyline, they crash out of the corral (one section was Balsa Wood) and all the cowboys chase after them. My horse, Hosteen, got his heel stepped on so I didn't go on to Wickenburg with the rest of the men. Oldsmobile was the other commercial in 1979 that they shot on the hill above the ranch.

A picture company from Mexico City filmed a feature *Revenge of a Killer* later that year. It was all in Spanish and they gave me a part where I talked to the star of the film. He didn't understand one word of English and I don't know Spanish, so they had to cue us both when we started our lines. They gave me words to say that made my lips believable when the lines are dubbed in Spanish. I was also the location manager for the Mexicans and furnished all the livestock, wagons and extras.

The television movie that year was called *Images of Indians* narrated by Will Sampson. It was a documentary showing how Indians were portrayed over the years in movies. Will Sampson used my horse, Hosteen, and believe it or not guessed his breeding. My stallion was King bred and Will recognized the breeding which was passed down to Hosteen.

In 1980, we only had one production, but it was an interesting one. We filmed two six-minute commercials for Cinevision in South Africa. Their product was Paul Revere Cigarettes, and they found out about me from an Arizona Highways Magazine they had picked up at a newsstand in Johannesburg. The magazine had one of my pictures in it. It was a double spread of the view from Bradshaw Hill and the caption was "The Most Beautiful Ranch Country Anywhere". When they telephoned me in Sedona, I told them I could get horses and cowboys for them. They put six of us local guys on camera and shot the commercials on 35-mm film.

The commercials were shown in theatres in South Africa. They had great action, great photography, great sound and great narration. There were only four people in the crew, Oliver Nurock, Producer, Jan Mastert, Art Director, Giacco Anguile, Grip, and Ashley Lazurus, Camera Director. They came up with a documentary approach of cowboy life that would take a 20-man crew in this country to produce. We showed it on the big screen in the local theatre and it was sensational. Many felt it was better than anything produced like it in this country. They were reproduced in black and white. Both of these commercials were six minutes long. At the end of the shoot, the director asked me to meet him downtown. I had no idea what he wanted. He then proceeded to take me into every store in uptown and told them that I was the best cowboy in the movie. Needless to say, that made my day.

While all of this filming was going on, the Bradshaw boys were getting bigger and still learning a lot about ranching.

In July of '81, the producer from WBEN radio station called me up and told me they had an idea for a commercial. It was a weird one in my opinion. The opening is two people walking out of an elevator in L.A. They imagine they are at Red Rock Crossing as they step out of the elevator. The filming in Sedona begins with the camera set up in the middle of Oak Creek facing Courthouse Rock. With cameras rolling, the girl on the elevator passes camera left on a sorrel horse, and the man passes camera right on his horse. They both come together in front of the camera and race through the water toward the scenery. I knew I was in trouble when the director called and said, "We've got this good actor who can really ride and he's taking riding lessons every day this week." They wanted him to ride a light colored horse like a buckskin or a palomino. So I said, "What if he can't ride this light colored horse. Do you want us to double him?" The director replied, "Oh, he can do it alright." So, the day came for the shoot and we got him on a bay horse. He couldn't get him out of a walk. We asked again, "Do you want us to double him or do you want him to ride a bay horse that will do it for him?" They then asked, "How do we know he can do it on the bay horse?" So, we put my 10-year-old son, John, on him and he went through the water like a racehorse. It was our horse, Star, who happened to love the water. When you show her what you want her to do once, she'll do it over and over again. So, we put the guy on Star and they rolled the cameras. When the actors got to the end of the run, there was a deep hole and the horses went out of sight. The two actors were up to their necks in water. This went on for quite a few takes. Star took the actor through every time and took him back to the starting point. All he had to do was hang on. The girl could ride pretty well, but after she made the run we had to get her horse and lead it back every time. I always wondered why these commercial people don't use local riders that can do the job.

In 1982, we did one commercial, one-feature story for Mademoiselle, and a BVD men's underwear ad. The commercial was for Durango chewing tobacco, a Beechnut product. We worked on Schnebly Hill and on Dry Creek, when Dry Creek was running. Their actor was wearing brown clothes and they wanted the horse to be bay or brown with a brown saddle and brown saddle blankets. I thought maybe they wanted it this way so that the tobacco juice wouldn't show in case the actor was to spit out some in the wrong place. We used Star for the cowboy to ride and she went through the water real fast. She loves to do water chases. While we were shooting it snowed, and we had to go to Cordes Junction for some of the shots without snow.

The feature story for Mademoiselle was shot entirely at Bradshaw Ranch. It appeared in the May 1982 issue. The BVD ad was photographed at the adobe house on Bradshaw Ranch. They used movie snow on the outside of the house and had their star throw some water out the door. Then we went to Taylor Tank where the wind was cold and very strong. The star was supposed to carry a bucket of water out of the pond. They had a space heater there and a canvas stretched over a fence. The wind was blowing so hard that the canvas was flying horizontally. The poor guy had to do his thing with just a cowboy hat and wearing his BVD shorts. After that, their final shot was the cowboy sitting on a bedroll in a cave in front of his campfire in his BVD's.

In 1983, we worked on a TV movie and a Sheplers catalog. The Sheplers catalog was photographed at Red Rock Crossing. Still ads for England's Marlboro and American Marlboro were shot at the ranch. Linda Carter's movie *Body and Soul*, a documentary on her life, was filmed in the Bradshaw Ranch area. All of the Marlboro men came to Sedona in 1983 and all of the photography (stills) were taken in the Bradshaw Ranch area.

Gambler II, starring Kenny Rogers, Linda Evans and Bruce Boxleitner, was filmed at Bradshaw Ranch and many other locations around Sedona. I showed Director, Dick Lowry, and his cameraman every location they used. Some of the locations included Bell Rock, Red Rock Crossing, Taylor Tank, Schnebly Hill, Foxboro Lake, Chavez Crossing and the Loop Road overlook. The 1879 movie set at Bradshaw Ranch was called *Jubilee* in the movie.

In 1984, we filmed *Thunder Warrior*, two Kodak commercials and Honda Bike commercial. *Thunder Warrior* was an Italian feature film production about the search for an Indian boy. The story involved 40 deputies using bloodhounds and a six-man horse posse and a search from the air. I got the bloodhounds, the horse posse and worked in the picture myself. Ed Wright and I were cast in small roles. In one scene, we rode our horses to the top of a hill and spotted the Indian below. My character spots the Indian, I shout, "There he is." and we point our guns at him. The director wanted us to shoot the guns, but we refused because they had a charge in them like a canon and we didn't want to injure the ears of our horses. With their special effects, they showed our guns going off. When the Indian fired back at us with a bazooka, there was a big cloud of smoke around us. My horse was upside down with his legs kicking around in the air. They must have had a mechanical prop horse to do this shot. The part of the movie filmed in Sedona was all done at Bell Rock.

The Kodak commercials filmed in 1984 were shot at Bradshaw Ranch and involved a motorcycle race. The commercial on the loop road showed a fat cowboy who lost his horse and was carrying his saddle. The bicycle guy came along to help him. Then they went back to Bradshaw Hill and filmed the bike rider talking to an old Indian.

Also in 1984, we worked on a magazine ad for Honda bikes. I posed on my horse, Hosteen, and the bike rider on the Honda came by. The locations were Taylor Tank and Boynton Pass.

The next three films, the State of Arizona Film Commission beat us out of and gave the location work, livestock work, and casting to someone else. I was in the film business for 25 years before they organized this commission. When I helped them get started up here in Sedona, I kept saying, "What will you do when you think you know it all up here." They said, "We will always call you". They cut me off many years ago and will not tell me why. The three features were *Dream West* with Richard Chamberlain playing Fremont, *The Quick and the Dead* with Sam Elliott and Kate Capshaw, and *Midnight Run* with Robert DeNiro, which most people don't realize had segments shot here in Sedona. It's rumored that DeNiro has a house here in the Red Rocks.

In 1985, I worked on another Marlboro commercial for Hong Kong. This time, two of the regular Marlboro men, Jerry and Billy, came to Sedona and left Daryl Winfield in Wyoming. I guess the Chinese client didn't like old cowboys. Daryl has, without a doubt, been on more billboards and television ads then any other person in history in America and overseas.

We had three companies photographing stills for ads and catalogs in 1986. We also worked that year on a Wells Fargo bank commercial. The commercial showed only in California, because that's where the bank was located at the time. Of course it has expanded its base of operations now. The commercial depicts an historic 1855 fire that wiped out the town of Grass Valley, California. The company called us to see if we had a period set and we told them we did. This was about the time we traded the south 40 acres of the ranch for 25 acres on the Loop Road through the Forest Service. They were very good about leaving the set there until we could afford to move it. Bitter Creek was getting pretty old and dilapidated. We found out that it would cost $50,000 to move it across the line to the section of the ranch we were keeping (90 acres). So when the production company called, we told them for $50,000.00, we would let them burn the building to the ground, not knowing that this is exactly what they wanted to do. They called back in a couple of days and said they were going to take us up on the offer. They built some additional sets (just fronts) to make the town look bigger and staged this spectacular fire, which burned everything down. The 30-second version doesn't show well, but the sixty-second version is a masterpiece.

In 1987, I worked on a still shoot for a Chevy 4x4 print advertisement. Next, I was hired as production manager for a German television production. It was a 6-hour mini-series called *All Inclusive*. The locations included Bradshaw Ranch, Submarine Rock, Red Rock Crossing, Los Abrigados Resort and the Village of Oak Creek. Because it wasn't very busy in the remainder of 1987, I had time to ranch, take photographs and do all of the other things I like to do.

A bunch of attorneys riding at the movie set

The trail ride north of the ranch with John on the center horse wrangling

In 1988 I was busy again. We worked on three Taco Bell commercials, a music video with Crystal Gale, a magazine layout for New Yorker magazine, and a still shoot for Nissan, Canada. I was the location manager for Rick Rusing photography. The first Taco Bell commercial was shot on the road to Bradshaw Ranch. The story of the commercial involved a party of young people in a big red stock truck riding along the road. They pass two girls on horses and the two girls chase the truck. Cindy Folkerson transferred from the horse to the truck. Then the truck goes to a Taco Bell Restaurant that is built for the shot on Boynton Pass Road. The second Taco Bell commercial was called *Run for the Money*. The actor is chasing a $100 bill and jumps over a wall where the wind blows the money. He doesn't know there is a bull on the other side. The bull chases him back over the wall. In the third Taco Bell commercial, a farm boy decides to leave his ranch and goes to Taco Bell in his red convertible.

In August of '88, we worked on a music video with Crystal Gayle. They shot scenes on Schnebly Hill and in Boynton Pass at the old Marshall Corral. I was responsible for the location work for Janet Flora of Flora Films, the company producing the video for Warner Brothers Music. In November of '88, I helped the Chrysler people scout locations. We also did a still shoot for Nissan Canada. New Yorker magazine asked me to find locations for them and I helped photographer, Al Satterwhite get a great shot.

In June 1989, we had a call from ARD German Radio and TV. They wanted me to appear in a documentary film on cowboys and talk about my experiences with western films. I agreed to work some cattle at the Woo Ranch, where we could have a great Red Rock background. When they arrived, John and I put the cattle in the pictures and we both rode up to be interviewed.

In '89, we also worked on the Judd's music video. Locations were Schnebly hill, the Woo Ranch, Red Rock Crossing and Boynton Pass. I also scouted out the locations for Frito Lay commercial. Locations were Long Canyon Road and Oak Creek Canyon switchbacks.

In November of '89, we had a Chevy Truck commercial with Momentum Productions. Chris Woods was the cameraman and E. J. Foerster, the producer. We worked at Hart Prairie, the Michelbaugh Ranch and the Swanson Ranch. Our last job in '89 was a commercial for Lee Jeans, England.

In 1990, we had a job with Blue Sky Pictures for a still shoot in a magazine ad for Volkswagen vans. In March 1990, we worked on a Marlboro shoot with Chuck Kuhn photography. I was the location man; they used Bradshaw Ranch, Long Canyon Road, and Boynton Pass. April 1990, I had a job with J.W. Thompson Agency. Ron Davis was the director. We used the Sally Wooster property in Dry Creek. It was a shoot with Ed Bruce as narrator.

After that, we organized a model shoot with Leslie Evans and Jackie Dressler. Most of the pictures were taken at Bradshaw Ranch. Also in 1990, we worked on a Nissan job with Zwart Studios. Locations were Deer Pass Ranch, Boynton Pass and Ray Steeles property. In November 1990, I was location scout for Charles Westerman who was shooting the Clydesdales for a Budweiser Beer calendar.

The 90's brought Linda, my fifth wife, into my life. You will see many photographs of her in the book. She was a good horsewoman and helped me a lot with the ranch. We did a lot of traveling and taking photographs in Utah, Colorado, Wyoming and Montana. These breathtaking photographs are part of the closing photographs in this book.

In 1993, we made a pilot for a television series at the ranch starring Beau and Lloyd Bridges. It was called *Harts of the West* and was very well done and exciting. They built a two-story set for the production on Bradshaw Ranch. About ninety percent of the picture was shot at the ranch. I used my Screen Actors Guild card to double Lloyd on horseback and was seen on the preview promo that went around the world. When the producer decided to move to California to shoot the series, it slowly went down the drain. The director said, "You go to California and I quit." Beau Bridges and his family still send me a Christmas card every year.

On May 20, 1996, Jim Brown from CBS came to Sedona to interview me at the ranch. He did a sensational job of floating in sequences of many of the old westerns we made here and discussing how it has now evolved into a Realtor-Tourist town.

Recently, my sons, John and Scott, have taken over the management of the ranch using it as a destination tour business and have made a few commercials of their own. The last one I can remember was a Subaru commercial starring Paul Hogan (Crocodile Dundee).

While my life seems perhaps to be measued by events of interest rather than by an intospective depth of experience, my approach to the context of my life has been a simple but powerful one. I see what I want and without consideration of how unreasonable it may seem, I totally focus on it...and usually get it. This quiet internal formula has been my secret for a life that, while not always approved of by everyone else, has been completely satisfying to me. It is a life I would live again and change nothing. And that alone I think is quite an accomplishment.

And now today I find myself in the twenty-first century reflecting back at the way Sedona was when I arrived here so many years ago. Times have changed, my family grew, and yet I somehow feel not much different. I still ride a horse, still do location scouting, and continue to take photographs of the land I love. I don't live on the ranch anymore, but the memories of my adventures there are still alive and hundreds of tourists visit the living archive of our life in the west every day with my sons' jeep tour company, A Day In the West.

My three sons all have children of their own now. Bob Jr. has three kids, Jami, Adam and Justin. John and his wife, Maree, have Jillian and Mason, and Scott has a daughter, Kylie. Jami's son, Shane, is my first great-grandson. I am proud of all of them.

I have outlived many of my contemporaries and expect to be around for quite a while yet to experience more of the wonder of this country I love so much. The Movie Museum in Uptown Sedona houses the history of my involvement in all of the Westerns made here in Northern Arizona. I look forward to the possibility of more movies that could be made here and hope that I can be a part of the making of them. One thing is certain. The movie of my own life has been worth the wild west ride I have been lucky enough to star in…the ending isn't quite clear yet, but I just might go out "ridin' the saddle" just like John Wayne did. I am grateful for all of the things, both difficult and wonderful, that have taken place through these years. And I appreciate the huge cast of characters that have touched my life and contributed to a life worth living in my beloved Sedona, Arizona.

John and Scott growing up on the Ranch . . .

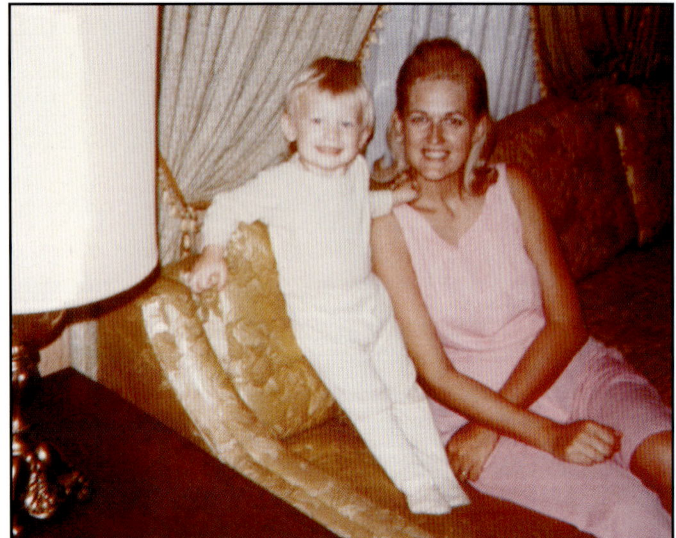

My son, John, and Marie

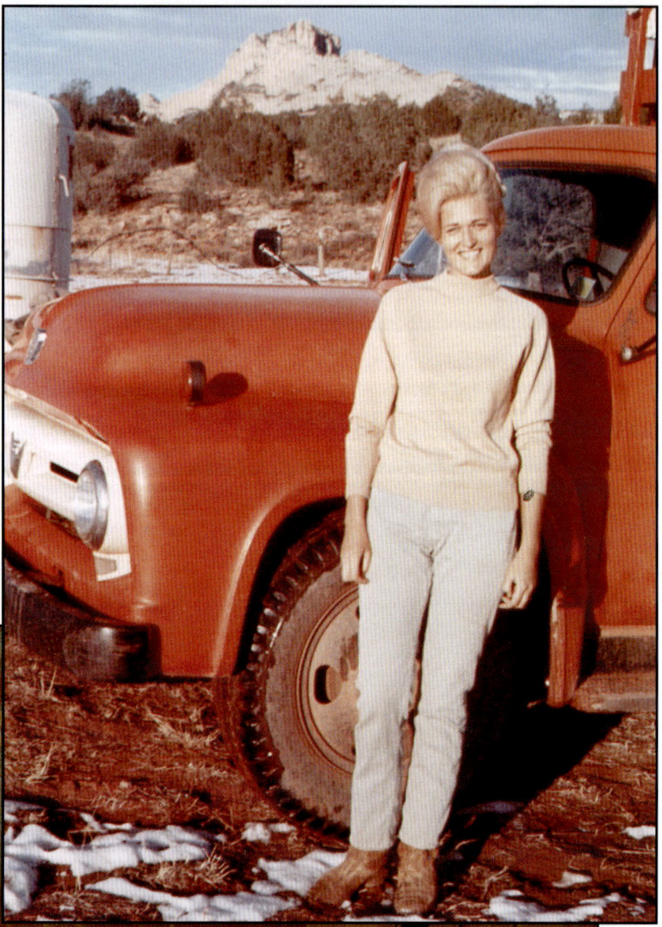

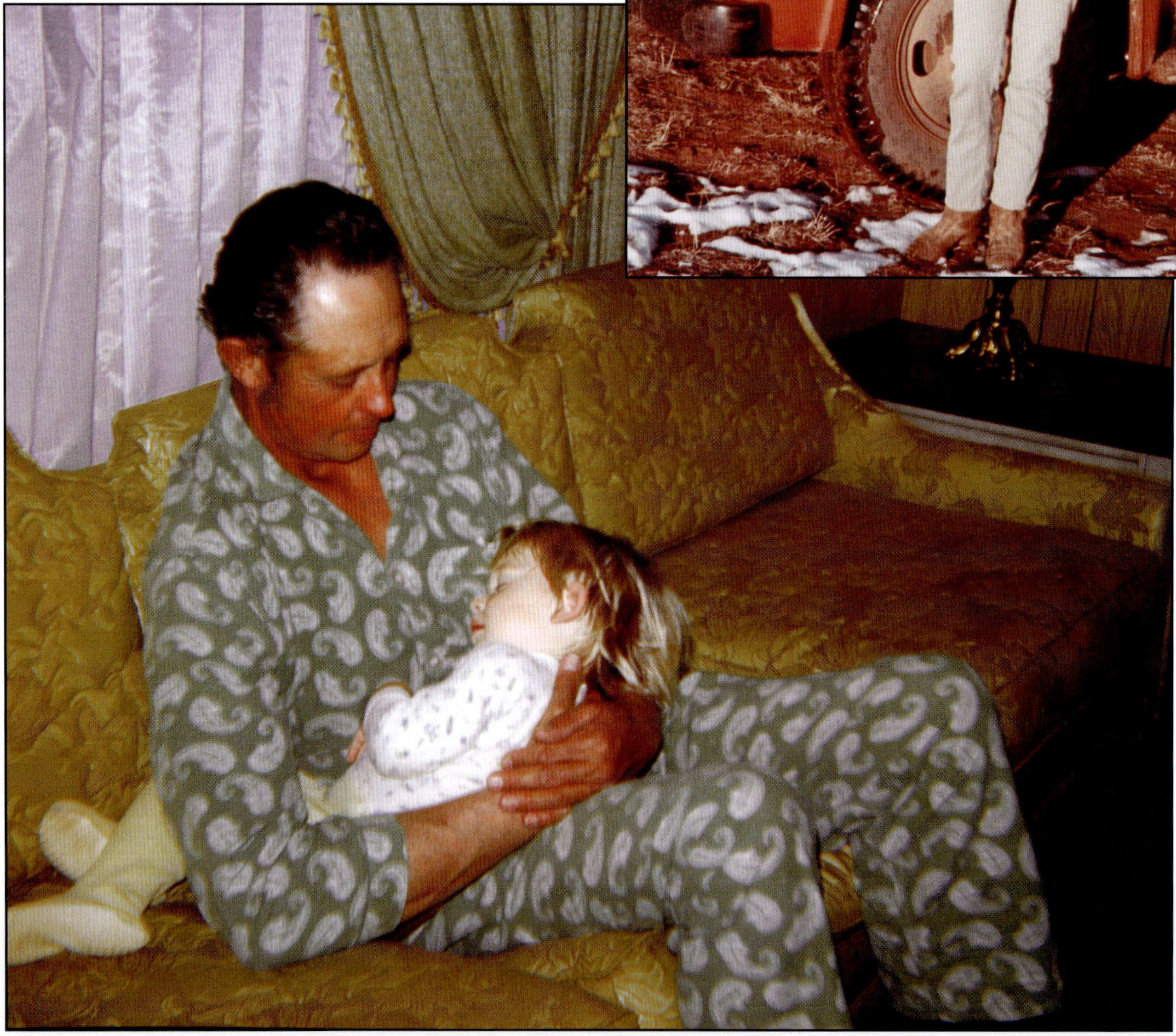

A tender moment with my son, John

John at four years old on Buck

Scott with colts

John is riding bareback above. John and Scott in Chinese garb and on a wagon as little cowboys below.

Top: John and Scott on a tractor

Bottom: John working the cattle

Scott on Buck

The boys driving cattle

Will Sampson with John and Scott

Scott and John riding through the movie set on Bradshaw Ranch

Bob Bradshaw Autobiography

Scott and John on their first trip to Monument Valley

John and Scott with new puppies at the ranch

NGAGI
MALE MOUNTAIN GORILLA
Gorilla g. beringei
BELGIAN CONGO
CAPTURED 1930 BY
OSA & MARTIN JOHNSON
DONATED 1931 BY
ELLEN B. & ROBERT SCRIPPS
DIED JANUARY 1944
WEIGHT 683 POUNDS
MODELED FROM LIFE BY
HOLGER & HELEN JENSEN
BRONZE DONATED BY
RACHEL L. WEGEFORTH

The boys on a turtle. They were wearing shirts that said Western Movie Trails.

Sea World in San Diego was a great adventure for my boys.

Flamingos at Sea World

The boys are watching the Dolphins

Scott at the ranch gate in the snow

Scott (above) and John (left) had already been riding horses for years. Scott, who is now a master mechanic and vehicle maker, by the age of nine, was already driving our truck on the open roads at the ranch and generally scaring the pants off of his older brother, John. Their crazy unsupervised antics while growing up on the ranch would make a great children's adventure book.

Bob Bradshaw Autobiography

A view of the Bitter Creek set on Bradshaw Ranch

The boys painting the corrals

John and Scott riding through the daisies

Part of our National Forest Service Cattle Ranch Allotment in Boynton Canyon

This is a trail that is west of the ranch.
Wide open country in the background,
everybody loved it.

John, bareback on
Hosteen, has just
made a fast run to
the top of the hill.

This is a trail we used to call Shotgun
Rock Trail - John is leading.

Bob Bradshaw Autobiography

John and Scott with a friend riding near the ranch

The boys at Taylor Tank

Me and my grandson, Adam

Adam is helping me round up these cows. He did a real good job that day.

Adam wrangeled cows with me all day.

Bob Jr.'s daughter, Jami and her son, Shane

Bob Jr.'s youngest, my grandson, Justin
on Bar Baby

John pushing a big bull in the canyon where *Angel and the Badman* was shot

John working cattle in Faye Canyon

I'm riding Gringo west of the ranch. Riding colts through rough country is good training.

My wife, Linda, and I riding at Robinson Tank.

Scott as a teenager

Riding customers taking the trail above the movie town

Linda wrangling at the ranch

Linda leading Star through yellow daisies

Scott and Autumn at the ranch

Linda and I at the top of the hill on the ranch

John on Gringo

John breaking a colt

This is the most beautiful canyon near the ranch. We would drive the cattle through here north in the spring and south in the fall. This is where *Angel and the Badman* starring John Wayne was filmed.

John's paint colt and his mother

Renegade and his mother on the day he was born – Loy Butte in the background

Renegade was born sorrel and turned white as he grew older – something I have never witnessed before or since.

Me riding Hosteen and ponying Renegade

My wife, Linda, punching cows at our waterhole on the ranch.

John and Me

John's shot of me – We were at Woo Ranch working cattle when we took each other's picture.

John tracking cattle near Taylor Tank

John married his high school sweetheart, Maree Giovannini, and started the next generation of Bradshaws. My grandchildren, Jillian and Mason, carry the adventurous Bradshaw spirit.

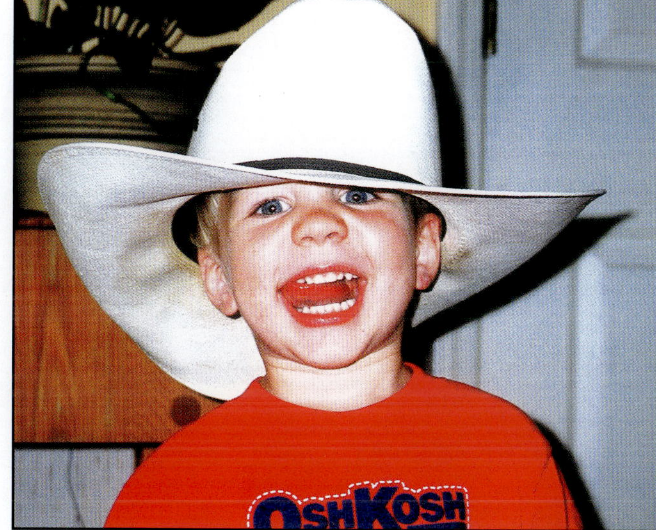

One day, Mason grabbed my hat and put it on. Kathleen captured the moment and made t-shirts from this photo for the whole family.

My Photographic Travels Outside of Arizona

The photographs in this section include some of the best scenes in our national parks. Most people familiar with my work are not aware of my photography outside of Arizona. I wanted to share these wonderful sites with you. These locations have warmed my heart as I hope they will yours. They are worth taking a trip to enjoy your own photographic experience. The rich color and the opportunity for interesting composition are demonstrated here for your pleasure. Even Monument Valley is not entirely in Arizona but is actually partially in the state of Utah. My scenic book, Indian Country, is dedicated solely to the extraordinary terrain of Monument Valley. During the era of the great western film classics, many features films were shot there in part or in their entirety. I was involved with the making of most of the movies in Northern Arizona, and my book, Westerns of the Red Rocks, contains that collection.

Yellowstone Park Prairies, Montana

Yellowstone Falls – Yellowstone National Park

Bryce Canyon National Park, Utah

Top: Moab, Utah

Bottom: Delicate Arch, Utah

Double Arch – Arches National Park

The Narrows – Zion National Park

Court of the Patriarchs above and the Great White Thrown below at Zion National Park

This scenic highway meanders through Wyoming

Teton National Park

Teton National Park

Oxbow Bend – Teton National Park

Jackson Lake – Teton National Park

Snake River Rapids – Teton National Park

The breathtaking views of the Grand Teton Peaks delights all scenic photographers.

Teton National Park
The best time to capture
this breathtaking
field of daisies is in
August when they are
in full bloom.

Teton National Park

The most beautiful
mountain country
anywhere.

Glacier National Park

The drive to Sun Highway is rich with beauty – Glacier National Park

Glacier National Park

Lake Mary – Glacier National Park

The Mittens at Monument Valley

This classic photograph
of me was captured one sunset in Sedona by Kathleen Francis
when we were taking some shots on Highway 179A.
Her work has complimented mine and it has been a pleasure
to have her support and share her talented writing skills.
Kathleen has helped to make my books more
than I ever imagined they could be.

©Kathleen Francis

Eldemira Portillo (Eldy) partner and camera assistant with Renegade

Flowers in Grand Teton National Park